*conversations
with my father,
adonis*

THE FRENCH LIST

conversations with my father, adonis

ninar esber

TRANSLATED BY LORNA SCOTT FOX

Seagull
BOOKS

LONDON NEW YORK CALCUTTA

Seagull Books

Editorial offices:

1st Floor, Angel Court, 81 St Clements Street
Oxford OX4 1AW, UK

1 Washington Square Village, Apt 1U
New York, NY 10012, USA

26 Circus Avenue, Calcutta 700 017, India

© Editions du Seuil, 2006
English translation © Lorna Scott Fox 2008

First published in English by Seagull Books, 2008

ISBN-13   978 1 9054 2 290 6

British Library Cataloguing-in-Publication Data
A catalogue record for this book is available
from the British Library

Typeset and designed by Seagull Books, Calcutta, India
Printed and bound in the United Kingdom at Biddles Ltd, King's Lynn

To Arwad
To Gabrielle
To Véronique H.
To Latifa, the daughter of Omar
And to every daughter who loves her father . . .

Contents

Foreword   ix

Forever Young   1

I Am What I Am   31

My Heart Belongs To Daddy   61

Lemon Inceste   77

It's A Man's Man's Man's World   91

Je T'aime Moi Non Plus   115

Rock the Casbah   131

Résiste   143

Stairway to Heaven   173

Heroes   191

Epilogue   221

Foreword

I wanted to do this interview with my father, Adonis, because I needed to get to know him and, most of all, to spend time with him. I wanted him to tell me things, to answer my questions. My questions as a 'daughter', his daughter, not as a journalist or an intellectual or a writer . . . I wanted to ask him simple questions and complex ones. With the right and freedom to ask things that were pointless, stupid, foolish, naïve or intelligent. Without censoring myself in any way. My questions arose independently of Adonis's poetic vision. They bear no relation to his writings; their link is to him, as a man, as a father, as a poet.

I should add that, in the course of our talk, my father came out with some of the classic responses and reactions of a father towards his daughter — something I didn't expect. Occasionally he tried to provoke me by playing devil's advocate, either to know my deepest thoughts or to force me to take sides, to commit myself.

I find it amusing that we had to resort to the subterfuge of the interview in order to have, at long last, a father–daughter relationship, and that I couldn't help thinking to myself at times: 'Well! That's a bit old-fashioned of him' or 'That's pretty macho!'

Today I have no regrets about 'the father's absence' all through my childhood and adolescence. It enabled me to develop my personality without impediments, even if such impediments may be useful.

When you grow up with a 'towering' image of the father who is not there, not around, it's like not knowing how to swim and seeing the vastness of the sea ahead and the land retreating under your feet and having no choice but to plunge in head first. You don't know which way to go, which position to take, you flail about swallowing water, unable to breathe, coughing and spitting — before eventually settling into your own pace and finding a direction.

And if along the way, among those waves, you find the father again, then it's a reward or a piece of good news, because somewhere along the road you'd forgotten where you were headed, and whether you were on your way to meet someone or not.

I feel as though I ultimately met my father through a studied kind of chance.

Forever Young
(ALPHAVILLE, 1984)

NINAR: *There is a saying, a silly one perhaps, but it haunts me, and I can't work out what it means: 'If youth but knew, if age but could.' Do you think that sums up the cycle of life? Isn't it really nonsense? What are the fundamental things one can no longer do as one grows old, and how should one manage one's youth?*

ADONIS: I believe that in one way or another, youth is linked to old age just as old age is linked to youth. But this kind of notion can hardly be applied in a blanket fashion. Each person's life is unique and particular. Each individual marks out a way for his life — a path — that he will or will not follow. In order to answer that question, you'd have to ask someone if they thought their personal life had a meaning. And what that meaning was. If someone thinks of his life as a tree, then the question will be irrelevant for him. Because he didn't choose to be born; he was flung into a world where he is tossed to and fro at the whim of coincidence and opportunity, buffetted by the winds of life . . . But if on the contrary this person thinks that his life means something, then he begins to feel responsible for it. So he tries to enhance it, to make it more free and to inscribe it into the world. Everything will be different from then on. The most important point, for me, is to say that a man is invited to construct his life or to not construct it. Therefore it depends on the person. As far as I'm concerned, it's as though my life had no meaning whatsoever outside writing, because writing helps me to understand myself and to understand the world I live in a little more; it enables me to live better, to push back the boundaries and provide an alternative vision which may be a help to those who are impressionable or too easily deflected . . . That is why I say that youth and age are bound up together. It's a perfect loop that ends with death. Sometimes not even then. Because a 'creator' may die but his work remains, his writings, his music, his thoughts and so on. His oeuvre becomes an integral part of the movement of life. Throughout human history, all great thinkers, philosophers, poets, painters have died, and still their works live on amongst us. They have physically passed away, yet they are with us. We read their literature, their poetry, we listen to their music, we communicate with them, they counsel and illuminate us . . . Creation is the mainstay of life. Even nature is engaged in perpetual creation; if you look at plants, flowers, rivers, floods, volcanoes, you'll see perpetual mobility, perpetual flux. Human life has that same mobility. The essence of a human being, it seems to me, is the capacity to create things greater than oneself. That's what distinguishes us from other living species, which are incapable of separating themselves from nature. For that reason they can't have a history, whereas man *is* able to separate himself from nature — he can even, in the abstract, separate himself from himself. He can domesticate nature, and this interactivity is what creates his history. The crucial thing, for me, is to live life to the full and to be constantly creating, in order to make life better. Especially as a man can die several times in a lifetime — he doesn't die only once! He can die if he experiences a great sorrow, poverty, betrayal, inactivity, et cetera. And he can also be reborn time after time, thanks to his infinite quest for creativity . . .

In that sense, then, there's no difference between youth and old age?

No, none in that sense . . .

It's a continuum . . .

There's a difference of degree. Age makes us more mature, in one way, and at the same time it returns us to infancy. We come full circle. In being born man emerges from nothingness, from death, as it were; as he grows older he nears death once more and the nearer he approaches to death, the nearer he comes to his origin . . . Death is another facet of life, and old age, another form of childhood.

You said that when a creator leaves a body of work behind him, it's a way of not dying, since our work outlives us, and yet I'm thinking: why should I care if my work lives on, when I'm not going to be around myself! It's like having children. As a rule—to make a long story short—people have them so as to leave something behind, a progeny.

Children are somewhat different . . . I'll go into that later. But I'd like to say one more word about death and the survival of an oeuvre. To be the contemporary of a particular artist or thinker can throw up a screen, like a barrier between you and that person's creation. You can't know it for what it is, you can't encompass it as a whole. Take a genius like Picasso, for example: you won't be able to get the measure of his work while he's alive; there can also be the obstacles of jealousy, rivalry, hatred . . .

There's not enough distance?

After the person's death, chances are we can understand him better. Because the veils fall away, leaving the work. Sometimes death has the power to throw light on a personality or a work   . . .

Are you saying we've got to wait for artists or any great creators to die before we can understand them?

It's the everyday law of this world . . . Life is a struggle in which the strong devour the weak, as they do in nature. There's no moral law that regulates things in nature. That said, there's not really a moral law for our lives either, even though men do their best to impose one. We know they don't always *succeed . . .*

Do you think it's possible to survive a father like you? Especially when the Arab world is in deep crisis, politically, religiously and intellectually? Overtaken by a stupid, destructive fanaticism? For me you represent a form of hope, a buffer against this 'decadence' of the Arab world, this Islamic fanaticism which is after nothing but the takeover of power. If you were suddenly not there, I get the feeling I'd be standing right in the path of that violence! I don't know how well equipped I may be to confront it, to dodge it or to under-stand it. That's why I like being in Europe—except when I see those fundamentalist lunatics in London with the right to say the most horrific things, or girls in Paris who absolutely insist on wearing the veil, on wrapping them-selves around in their chains while other girls in Arab or Muslim countries are fighting and risking their lives to take off the veil, or at least not to have it forced upon them. Europe itself is not exempt from fundamentalism, in the sense of its extreme right-wing movements. Luckily there are laws in Europe, the states are strong, France is a secular country (let's hope it remains one forever!) and a democracy. For all its faults, I feel safe here.

As the situation is now . . . But if you look at history, Europe was going through dark times, without laws or security, at a period when the Arabs were much more advanced than the Europeans. Historical eras vary according to political and sociological change . . . If fundamentalism is thriving today, it doesn't mean that the world is coming to an end and fundamentalism will rule the roost for evermore. Fundamentalism is not to be explained by its strength but by the weakness of the forces that have failed to oppose it.

There's nothing to draw people elsewhere.

There's no other option. Faced with fundamentalism, there's only weakness, indifference and disarray . . . Such deficiencies, both in society and at the level of the state, make fundamentalism seem all-powerful and omnipresent. But it's not really like that. If the struggle against fundamentalism is feeble or virtually non-existent in today's Arab world, it's largely due to the deteriorating social situation, and a shocking economic and intellectual poverty. There are historical reasons, too. The way governments and dictatorships have taken power over individuals, over their spirit, their body, their dreams . . . In a context like that, a person feels completely hobbled, like a prisoner . . . We shouldn't regard it as a definitive or permanent situation. But to return to your question concerning me: I think that life abandons and transcends everyone, whatever their importance or their 'greatness', whether they be father, friend, president or poet. All the 'greats' of history have been transcended by life . . .

It may have transcended them, but —

Physically, I mean.

Yes.

And life doesn't stop for all that. That's how survival is possible. A father has to survive the death of his own father, and then sometimes the death of his son . . . Death must be accepted as forming part of life. If my father dies, I don't die along with him; on the contrary, I must take on his strength and follow his example, struggle as he did, and give a meaning to his struggle . . . If I were to die after him, it would be of no use. The power of life lies in the way it transcends everything. And that's also the greatness of man. Man forms part of History, and yet he can transcend History . . .

How do you think I should confront or get through this dark period? Do you really think it's a 'decadence'?

Yourself, do you mean?

Yes, yes . . .

You and your generation both . . . In order to be strong, you'd do well to be or to remain yourselves, because a weak person can't fight back and has no role to play in society. So you have to work, and construct yourselves. To do that, you must enter into and cultivate a relationship with the world around you. Someone who doesn't produce does not exist as a person, and feels that they do not exist. That's why as soon as you feel capable of producing something, you know you're contributing to the onward march of the world, taking part in the construction of the world. Your strength will stem from there, and no one will be able to take it away from you, no one will be able to undermine you . . .

Can you imagine if your father were alive in these times? Can you picture him chatting and living in the village? Or in Damascus? How do you think he'd react to the Syrian regime, to religious fanaticism – a man who was made a sheikh[1] as a tribute to his wisdom and his vast knowledge of the Koran and of Arab culture?

1 Title awarded in the villages to a man in honour of his advanced age or deep religious learning. In Arabic, 'old man'.

My father dwells in my mind, even though I never really knew him . . . I left the family home when I was little, and he died very young . . . I was away when it happened. However, I clearly remember that he never told me what to do. His advice was always to reflect before acting or taking a decision. 'After careful consideration, you can make up your mind. But never do anything without thinking it through beforehand.' That's all he ever told me . . . I treated your sister Arwad in the same way. One day she came along and said she wanted to join a political party. I said: 'I'm not opposed to your wish, but before you decide, get to know them; spend time with them, find out what they're like, what their views are, what they're doing, and then you'll be able to make an informed decision.' She came back a few months later and said to me: 'I wasn't convinced, so I've changed my mind!' My relationship with my father still torments me. I didn't know him well enough, and when he died I didn't weep . . . I don't know why . . . But the more time goes by, the more I think about him and the closer it brings me to tears. I'm coming to realize what a friend he was. He was not a good father, being rather harsh and strict, but deep down he was as kindly as a friend. I only understood this after he was gone . . . and how I reproach myself for it! Now I'm very grateful, and faithful to that light I glimpsed in him. Even if I never talk about him, he inhabits me. Sometimes I try to conjure him up, I think about his being, his friendliness . . . He is here, with me. Even if I don't agree with his opinions or share his worldview, a profound mystery joins me to him. It gives me strength, it inspires me to question quite a number of things, and to be judicious in my choices. He shines like a light inside me. And this inner light doesn't fade—no, the more I advance through life, the bigger and brighter it becomes . . . Curiously enough, I'm forgetful of a lot of things, images and even faces. But I'll never forget the last image I have of him. It's as if he was standing there in front of me. What would he be doing today? I think he'd be at home, reading or perhaps writing, too, because he was himself a poet . . . One remarkable aspect of my father was the forcefulness of his character. He was steely, he never gave way . . . Sometimes he'd be alone in standing up to someone, a regional governor or political boss. Everyone would go out to salute this powerful figure and he'd stay at home, as a mark of indifference or opposition. When I was a boy I went with all the villagers to greet the then President of the Republic, Shukri al-Kuwatli,[2] because I wanted

2 Shukri al-Kuwatli (1891–1967): first president of the Syrian Republic after independence and the end of the French mandate (1943–49). Re-elected in 1955, he governed until 1958.

11

to recite a poem I'd written for the occasion, bidding him welcome and asking him to help me go away to school and study. My father did nothing to stop me. I was barely thirteen. And yet the festivities had been organized by the governor of the Jable[3] region, who heartily disliked my father, and the feeling was mutual! Despite this, he said: 'Go, and may God keep you, good luck; but I refuse to go.' Those are things I'll never forget, and to this day I find it hard to fathom such a generous gesture, so telling of his wisdom and his respect for me and my dreams.

He was awarded the title of sheikh — how did that happen?

Well, it wasn't hereditary, but in honour of his wisdom. He was a sage, a highly cultured and scholarly man; they made him a sheikh out of respect for his learning and his great goodness.

Who gave him the title?

The notables, the intellectual and religious leaders . . .

[LATER . . .]

Not long ago you quoted me a line from Abu Ala'a al-Ma'ari,[4] in which he asks one who is walking to walk slowly, because he is stepping on the bodies of people, animals and insects.

'Walker, take care as you step, tread more lightly, cease trampling the earth that is woven from the bodies of men . . .'

3 Small town on the Syrian coast, the nearest centre to Adonis's native village.

4 Abu Ala'a al-Ma'ari (973–1057): Syrian poet, born in Ma'arrat al-Numan near Aleppo; blind from the age of four; famous for his critique of religion.

He's talking about men! I thought it was about animals and insects!

No. Human beings.

I'd understood it wrong, then. You quoted the lines during our lunch with some friends of yours at Kefraya,[5] in Lebanon. We were talking about animals and I said how shocked I was by certain religious traditions, rituals like the sheep sacrifice for the feast of Al-Addha;[6] and then, more generally, by the type of person who goes in for what they call 'big game in a tin', in Africa, in Namibia to be precise.

What is that?

There are these farmers in Namibia who make money by setting up nature reserves full of lions, giraffes, gazelles, elephants and whathaveyou. They get billionaires to come and hunt on their land for fifty thousand dollars. These hunters, who are cowards, trap lion cubs in order to lure the mother who comes looking for them . . . There she is, a few yards off from the hunter who's standing tall in his jeep armed with his fantastically sophisticated rifle . . . She is riddled by one, two, three, four, five shots . . . She staggers to her feet to protect her young . . . The hunter blasts her again! Absolute slaughter! They play the same trick on elephants and giraffes . . .

Hisham Sharabi[7] says that when mankind stops killing animals for food, then we can start talking about humanism. He's got a point, hasn't he?

I feel very passionate about animals and trees. It must be because of Beirut and the war. I spent fifteen years of my

---

5 Small Lebanese village renowned for its winery (Château Kefraya).

6 Major Muslim festival that concludes the pilgrimage to Mecca, better known as Eid el-Kebir.

7 Hisham Sharabi (1927–2005): Arab thinker of Palestinian origin; lived in the United States and wrote at length on patriarchal Arab society. Died in Beirut.

life without a sight of animals anywhere but in films or on TV (I tell a lie: once I saw a calf in the village). In Beirut, the only creatures I saw close up were the chickens at the butcher's! And the fighting cocks bred by the neighbours at the back of our building . . . People who were living on a sort of waste patch of red earth, where they had built this little two-storeyed house. It was temporary, illegal. It lasted for years. My bedroom balcony overlooked it. Every Sunday they'd bring out their roosters, the guests arrived with their own birds, and the battles began. I could hear the screams of the poor beasts and was helpless to do anything. The defeated cock covered in blood would seek out its owner and he, furious at having lost money and face, would kick it away from him . . . And of course the sheep, the ones whose throats would get cut on feast days. I used to see them from the car, all tied up and numbered . . . People fed them, children threw stones at them or stroked them . . .

I think I was traumatized by this violent relationship to animals. Not to mention all those cats run over by cars, eyes staring, jaws crushed. Or the fact that there wasn't a single bird left in the sky or on the trees, but you'd find one, maybe, on a plate!

On winter evenings, when the aerial bombing let up at the end of the day before coming back with a vengeance late at night, I used to hear tiny mewings in the darkness, coming from deserted or gutted buildings. I wondered what it was, and soon realized that the sounds were either kittens calling their mother (feeling hungry or scared), or a mother cat searching for her frightened babies in the dark. Because those sounds were nothing like the yowls of a cat on heat, or the territorial noises they make . . . I longed to protect them, to comfort them, as I could feel and understand their panic. I was just as distraught as they were, afraid of dying and especially afraid that my parents might die . . . So I'd go down at night with my mum and feed them some cheese, 'The Laughing Cow' or something . . . Even now, when I'm in Beirut and come across any street cats, I can see the fear in their eyes when they're trying to cross the road, between big cars and hurrying people. The cat looks terrified, eyes wide, ears flattened back, ducking his head left and right as he tries to weave a way through. Whenever I see that it makes me want to cry, imagining what's going on in his mind . . . The lack of contact with any animals living peacefully left its mark on me.

All too much violence. And of course I saw people die, friends executed, assassinated, killed by the shelling, children terrified or injured. But the children, thanks to the solidarity that war creates, were kept close by their parents and, if the parents were absent or dead, most children would be taken in by relatives or neighbours, or even passing strangers. A child was comforted and protected (as far as possible, because I learned much later that it's illusory to think you can protect anyone during a war). Old people were cared for in the same way.

Many children used to play at war, as though to exorcize the surfeit of violence. Parents would explain the reasons for the deafening crash of a shell hitting a building, the blast that preceded or followed the explosion and could lift up a child or an adult and slam them against a wall, into the furniture, through a window, whatever. And then the smoke everywhere, the thick scent of gunpowder, that unbreathable smoke . . . And me always worrying about the cats! What can you say!

I was desperately keen to have pets at home, to keep them safe and minister to their every need. I had cats, and lots of baby chicks. But when they got bigger they were taken away and it shattered me. They had to be sent god knows where, to some person's house which supposedly had a yard full of other chickens! Everyone lied, telling me how happy and free they'd all be together and how they'd die of old age. But I knew jolly well they'd end up on the plates of the people who took them. I just didn't have any say in it. I remember one little hen I was particularly fond of—when the time came for us to part I painted red nail varnish on her claws, so I could 'recognize' her when I went to visit!

I had some pet silkworms, too. It was quite an education for me, coming to terms with the death of the adult moths. I remember how traumatized I was at first . . . Those little worms I'd bred, so cute, the noises they made munching through the mulberry leaves I used to bring them . . .

We really don't have to fight nature in order to survive nowadays. Since we dominate nature, we should be looking after it, not wrecking it. I know that as soon as money or profits are involved, people are ready to sell their mothers. Anyway, I always try to be positive, clinging fast to the hope that not all humans are murderers at heart (just kidding!).

Of course these things are dreadful, I agree, but men are also killing one another! You're right to feel that way about animals, and I do too. I believe we should oppose people who harm animals and nature, but, as you know, humanity everywhere is founded on sacrifice . . . In the olden days, the loveliest young girls were offered up in sacrifice . . . Be that as it may, such customs or habits must be fought.

Yes, it's not because something is a tradition that it should be kept up for ever and ever.

Those traditions are obviously reprehensible, and animals should be protected. And yet hunting can sometimes be useful for the management of species. If certain species are left to multiply without control, they can devastate the natural environment. But one mustn't make animals suffer, or kill them for the pleasure of killing. Actually, caring for animals is also a tradition within Islam.

Really?

The poet Abu Ala'a al-Ma'ari was a vegetarian. He didn't eat animal flesh, out of respect and love for all creatures . . .

What do monotheistic religions think about animals? That they are God's products, created to be eaten by man?

There's nothing wrong with raising an animal for its skin or its meat. It might even be regarded as a kind of reward . . .

During that lunch I mentioned, one of your friends said that when man starts protecting animals, and stops consuming them, then maybe we could start talking about humanism —

There's a case to be made for that position. But, on the practical level, it may well be impossible to implement. The world's population is steadily growing and before long, considerable numbers will run short of water and food. The world is heading for deep trouble. Hence the laws in some countries to limit the birth rate. Natural resources are going to become scarcer — it's a serious problem.

Do you think it's a matter of scarce resources? I don't agree, because the rich countries, the great powers, go to war to rob the things they need — water, oil, minerals, whatever — from poorer and less powerful countries. The whole of human history is built on wars of this kind. So it's not about whether there are enough resources. In any case, tough, strict laws could be introduced to save energy . . . In the meantime, powerful countries that are short of water prefer to steal it from their neighbours. There is a will to survive among the human species — why can't we have a firm will, enshrined in law, for the survival of animal species?

An animal is a living being, and life, in all its diversity, demands to be preserved. Although some people go rather too far in that respect. They won't eat any plants which possess, in their view, animal characteristics. I even read somewhere about plants that develop a relationship with the person who cultivates or looks after them . . . The plant becomes accustomed to the hand that gives it to drink, and sometimes it wilts, or gradually dies, if another person comes and waters it . . .

Oh, I totally believe that! For instance, when I go away for a few days I let my plants know . . . If I'm in a hurry, I'll talk to the banana tree . . . I tell him I'm going to be away for a few days. He's in charge, I know he'll pass the message on to the others! There was this study presented on the Discovery Channel two years ago, which showed how trees feel pain when they're attacked and not only that, they send out distress signals to other trees!

And what about carnivorous plants! They sit with open jaws, waiting for their prey, a butterfly, say. As soon as the butterfly lands, it is gobbled up! We might well speak of death here, to say that death is a part of life. Death by devoration or murder forms part of natural processes, although I think one should do one's utmost to avoid killing a living creature . . .

I feel the same way. For me, killing a butterfly for no purpose, just for the fun of it, opens the door to killing a man, just for the fun of it! Mind you, the opposite doesn't apply . . . People who are kind to animals are not necessarily kind to other people.

[NEXT DAY . . .]

What's your relationship like with your brothers and sisters? Is it easy to get on with them, or has a rift opened up

19

between you due to poetry, or to distance? Can 'family ties' make up for that distance?

One has to distinguish between brothers and sisters, cousins and the family.

I have many relatives I've never met, whom I don't know. Thus my dealings with them can only be superficial, a kind of acquaintanceship at best. As for my brothers and sisters, with them my relationship is inevitably different. I've lived with them, I am connected to them, it's a bond of love and affection. If they are ever in need and I'm able to help, I do so; they are part of my life . . . Even if there's no 'intellectual' affinity between us, even if they don't like my poetry, the mere fact that we're siblings, that we share the same mother, means I have a responsibility towards them. I try to imbue them with a little of myself, of my capabilities, so they can stand up to life, and learn . . . The same goes for my parents and other close family.

In my case, I had great trouble finding my feet among that family at first. It took me a while to adjust. If I hadn't been prepared to compromise, it would have been hopeless . . . I was always watching what I said, in case I upset them. At the end of the day I still feel unable to talk freely with them. I expect there's a price to be paid for that, a kind of isolation. However, I rely a lot on my friends. Some of those friends are my real family, the family I've chosen, cherished, protected, and sometimes even abandoned . . .

Only because you don't know your blood family! You've never lived with them, day in, day out. I suspect you'll feel differently one day. The more you advance through life, the more you'll have a sense of something lacking: the countryside, the village, your ancestors . . . All these are a part of you. For the time being, in view of the context in which you live and the experiences you've been through, life has carried you away from them. But you'll feel differently one day.

Are you saying I've got no choice? That it'll happen and that's that?

I take it to be a good thing, even on the social level, to come together with the people, that is, the background to which in the final analysis we belong. It is very important to meet them, to know how they think and live, to see them regularly . . .

Yes, maybe, on one condition: that the countryside will still be around! That the 'background' will not have turned into a concrete, treeless city! Besides, I'm not too keen on this notion of people always going back to their roots. I believe we can each evolve and create our own world.

When I say it's important to return to one's roots, I'm not implying that one should just leave it at that! I don't mean to say that one must stop there, and simply merge. On the contrary, a man has a duty to invent a new world, or at least should never give up on the possibility of doing so. The return I speak of can help us to measure the distance between ourselves and our beginnings and, by the same token, help us to know ourselves . . . In fact, this 'return' is a tool in the edification of a new world. A 'return' to the future!

Meanwhile I've got a family other than the one constituted by you, Arwad and Mother. It's a family made up of my very close friends.

I don't think they can replace your family. They can be *like* a family, as companions, as friends . . . You share common interests, spiritual and intellectual affinities, and yet there's something to do with the body, with history, with blood, that has nothing to do with friendship. It's something that cannot be learnt. You have to understand it.

Maybe so, but for now I see friendship as an alternative. How do you expect me to feel a sense of belonging to a community I have nothing in common with — different opinions, different lifestyles . . . ?

That's beside the point. You can easily agree with someone's ideas while knowing that you don't really belong to the same world as them. I know many people with whom I feel intellectually in sympathy, yet I could never coincide with their way of life.

I see what you mean, but if you won't sit down for a meal with them it's because they're 'heavy' or obnoxious. There's no reason why just because you click with someone's ideas you should be at one with them on everything. It takes more than that. You can't be friends with everyone, you go for the people who strike the most sympathetic chord — it could be those with whom you feel physically at ease, or whose thinking and life principles are congenial, or who have a similar spirit of fun or friendship. It's a whole mixture of things . . .

Take your family, back in the village. They represent a way of being you ought to find out about. It's a life experience that can be enormously enriching . . .

I agree with you wholeheartedly on that.

This family — your kin, as it happens — represents an aspect of life that can be enriching regardless of the fact that you're related. No one else can transmit that kind of insight to you.

In fact, you must get to know them — the better to know yourself. You'll never be able to grasp the distance that separates you, or for that matter the link that unites you, unless you know them well . . .

There are some members of our family I might feel a link with: my cousins and nieces who went abroad to continue their studies, Marwan, Mada and Alida . . . They know what it's like to be cut off from their friends, their home country, their culture. I can feel close to them, because I had the same experience.

Yes, but that's an emotional, subjective attitude. You see them as allies —

Of course!

But it's not necessarily so, for this is a superficial complicity, not a complicity of the heart. You must look more deeply. You on your side are making one thing of your distance from home, while they're making another of theirs. And so, in reality, you are different . . .

Fair enough, but if you tell me we're different when we have at least one thing in common, what's left for the people with whom I've got nothing in common at all!

That shared experience attracts you because it reassures you, and makes you think they're like you . . .

Exactly . . .

They, like you, went away, but it's only a stage; one day they'll go home, and then what will happen?

We'll still have that experience in common.

And if they go back to settle down in their country, where does that leave you?

Don't forget that when you travel or live abroad, you become transformed (or at least people with the will and the brains for it do). You start questioning your assumptions, you observe new things, you have new experiences, you grow, you change . . . That's how it's been for me so far, and maybe it'll be different when I'm seventy, but for the moment I find experience and constant discovery more valuable than things that are pre-ordained.

What I'm going through here in France (it could have been anywhere, of course) is pretty intense. I've become another person, or perhaps the same person but with a broader, hungrier mind . . .

What on earth am I supposed to talk about with a family I so seldom see? I'm happy to listen to them, but I very soon feel lonely in their company. The country is a new place for me, totally unfamiliar and weird however much I love the nature there, the animals and plants . . . And we do communicate about that. But it's not long before the limits of any conversation become apparent; we can only go so far on both sides.

I could never tell them about myself, for instance, about my outlook on life, animals, love, things in general . . .

Must you? Talk to them about yourself?

Of course I must, or else I'll start feeling isolated.

Well, I never shared much with my brothers and sisters. They have their way of thinking and I have mine.

Exactly, that's just what I'm trying to say! But you're someone who speaks very little about himself—you'll talk politics or poetry but hardly ever about yourself. Because you say it all in your poems, perhaps, but also because you don't need to talk. I've watched you, you have an aura, a presence that makes way for silence . . . You never have to say a word. Or only when you're performing. You're there, and that's all there is to it.

The villagers come to you, they're the ones who call on you. Every now and then you'll recite a couple of lines of verse, you'll drop a remark or two and it's enough to make an impression. The magic of your presence and your seductive charisma take care of the rest . . . But you're an unusual case. Things can obviously never work like that for me.

They will, with time . . .

Yes, and it's conceivable that my own priorities will change.

I am sure that's what will happen. You can't not love the country some day.

But I do love the country, that's not the point!

If you sit down in a wood and gaze at nature, it'll take at least three days before you begin to see the birds, understand how they build their nests, hear the sounds of the wind, see the sky and the glittering stars . . . You'll observe the trees, all in a row, side by side, but each completely unlike its neighbours. Sometimes they embrace, sometimes they quarrel . . . One of them may take another's water . . . They live in a community, like an image of our society in miniature. They are like human beings seated around a table, each helping himself to what he wishes to eat. You'll notice the tranquility of nature, the quiet of the night . . . This solitude will bind you to the earth, to nature and to the universe, more than a city ever could. Because a city exists in industry, not in nature. And mankind needs nature . . . The first time I went into a town, I was instantly overwhelmed, like you, by the desire never to have to return to my rural backwater. As though if I did, it would be like having to climb down into a tomb! And then, with time, I began to feel the reverse. Nowadays, it's like emerging from the grave to go towards nature.

[A FEW MINUTES LATER . . .]

Tell me more about you and your siblings. Were they jealous of you? And you? Were you jealous of them? Did you fight? How did you behave — like the head of the family, or like a spoiled child?

Neither.

What did you do? Did you work in the fields? Grandmother told me that you had a terrific temper, that you'd fly off the handle for the least thing and then you'd tear up the crops, out of spite . . .

I can't remember those days any more . . .

Can you say anything about the years when you were poor? I know it's something that scarred you for life, because you passed that anxiety on to us . . . I remember when I was eleven or twelve, you started to put the fear into me by saying that if I didn't work I was going to end up on the street, with no help from anyone . . . Not from my parents or my sister, and certainly not from my friends . . . And I still feel nagged by that anxiety, even if it didn't actually scare me into working my head off so as to make money or be shielded from the problems of life. It remains as a worry, sterile but crippling. On the contrary, I chose a path that doesn't exactly guarantee my material well-being.

So, just for once if you would, tell me in more detail or depth about that anxiety that has never let go of you.

I find it terribly difficult to talk about. But whatever I've said in that respect is rooted in personal experience.

Don't you think that exile is an opportunity? Despite all the grief it brings, the bottomless sensation of solitude, the loss of familiar bearings and of all easy givens . . . Being abruptly torn up and flung down in some new place, with a new language, new culture, new faces . . . I think it can be an opportunity, if one knows how to seize it. It's far more painful to feel like an exile in one's homeland, or in one's native language; I feel that that could drive one to suicide or madness.

Oh no, it's a very useful and constructive situation to be in. Artists, thinkers, poets—all those who have something to say and are possessed by the need to create—are exiles by definition. Exiles within their society, or even within their mother tongue . . . In order to create, one must always try to break new ground, within the realm of language or colour . . . Creativity is a banishment in itself, in that sense. The creative person is always in exile. And for that reason creators aren't burdened by it. It lies within them . . . This doesn't hold for other social categories: a Lebanese or Syrian labourer, say, or a shopkeeper, who emigrates to the United States. He spends twenty or thirty years of his life miles away from home, and yet his one dream is to go back to the land of his birth. He doesn't mingle with the host society . . .

He may even found a new 'Syria', or a new 'Lebanon', on American soil or wherever he happens to be!

Of course, and in that light exile no longer means a thing. The person who is conscious of being 'exiled' is one who knows that he must transcend this condition. The sensation of exile is a very potent one, and it's not given to everyone. It is a somewhat rare feeling.

Especially if this feeling relates to one's own country, one's language, one's body . . . And you? Where would you locate your sense of exile?

All my life, I've felt that the path I was engaged upon was a path of exile. Ever since my time in Syria, I've felt like an exile: an outsider in my village, in society, in the literature and modes of thinking of the day. I was always on the periphery — never at the centre, but out on the edge, and this is how I was able to make things that were different. It has shaped the very movement of my life: from the country to the city, from the city to the capital, and from Damascus to Beirut. And inside Lebanon itself I was always wandering from one province to another, from one home to the next. My whole life has been a long journey towards and within exile . . . And this exile has left its mark on my language, Arabic. I am an exile on this island we call the Arab tongue . . .

To what end?

So as to move off the beaten track; to bring together the conditions that enable me to do something different. Not something that flows with the current, in the mainstream[8] but something that goes against the grain . . .

I Am What I Am

(GLORIA GAYNOR, 1983)

NINAR: *What are you dependent on, what's your 'addiction'?*

ADONIS: Writing. Let me say it again: when I don't write, I feel as if I don't exist. Through writing I find out who I am, I learn to discover and to disclose myself . . . It also enables me to know others, and of course to know the world. I have the feeling that my whole life is an everlasting movement of discovery. It's that movement which makes a man feel alive, as a participant in the making and remaking of the world. And what can be said of poetry can just as well be said of all the creative forms, art, philosophy, everything.

How do you relate to your image, the image that others reflect back to you? How do you deal with it? Some regard you as a menace, others as a 'star', for some you are a 'visionary' and for others you're no less than a 'traitor'. . . You are both loved and hated. Does that frighten you?

If I were loved by all the world, I would have serious doubts about myself! Such a consensus would imply that I'm a superficial person, and that my work has failed to raise any questions or to stimulate controversy. Whenever I do unleash a storm of objections, it gives rise to one camp of people who like me and sympathize with my ideas and another camp of people who loathe me. Then I feel I'm on the right track . . . But to be honest I'm not particularly interested in what anyone says about me, good or bad.

Your ideas don't seem to have provoked much controversy in France or Europe. How do you account for that? Over here you're seen as an Arab poet, who can be expected to hold unusual opinions . . . Unless you too have fallen victim to 'political correctness'! Perhaps the main mission of a public intellectual is to think for most people, not on behalf or instead of them, but for them. If you turned into a polemical writer, a controversy artist, you'd probably start neglecting your art, wouldn't you? You'd become the artist on his soapbox, taken up with the externals, always trying to show off.

I couldn't agree more!

Given that you're a public figure, people tend to project their fears and failings, pettiness and generosity, complexes and frustrations onto you . . . You are a 'father figure' for several generations. Some acknowledge this and others persist in denying it.

I find that completely natural. There's nothing very surprising about such behaviour, to my mind. It shows that I'm not sitting still, I'm actively getting on with things regardless of any positive or negative reactions. Indeed, it gives me more strength, energy and self-confidence. In the same way, I never hesitate to help someone if I'm in a position to do so. I've never attempted to exploit my status to harm anyone, not even those who have behaved badly towards me . . . I am, I must say, astonished by this capacity I've acquired over the years to refrain from wronging or damaging others. I have often been the target of virulent attack, but if someone's criticism has a genuine point to make then I accept it as a criticism, and if I must respond then I try to do so within the rules.

Violence is generally the weapon of cowards and weaklings! People are aggressive as a substitute for inner strength. But you — you've no need to resort to violence. The fact that you exist, that your poetry exists, is a strength in itself and, at the same time, violence enough against those who have it in for you!

Sometimes it's very difficult to remain steadfast under this kind of critical barrage. Especially as such attacks are often deliberately designed to cause as much damage as possible. But somehow, I'm not sure how, I've always risen above these vindictive attacks, dangerous as they are. For they can often be deadly . . .

Some critiques are absolute lethal weapons . . .

Still, a man who has something to say and a purpose to his life carries on regardless.

I don't see you stopping and glancing behind you every five minutes!

It's no good getting involved in arguments with people who are not worth it. If you stoop to their level, you're only overstating their importance.

If they had anything serious to say, they wouldn't waste their time talking rubbish . . .

And I don't waste my time answering back. In fact, I never respond to someone who has insulted me.

[SOME HOURS LATER . . .]

Your first name is Ali and your writer's name is Adonis. Adonis seems to have taken over . . . What space is left for Ali? Does Ali ever feel invaded? Does he ever seek to escape from the pressures imposed by Adonis? Does he never rebel? Or are Ali and Adonis by any chance one and the same person?

I see no contradiction between Adonis and Ali, perhaps because my first name helped to eliminate it. The name Ali derives from 'El', the supreme god of the Sumerians. El, Elias, Ali, Adonis, they all mean 'my lord': all these words derive from the same root. I dare say this helped to resolve any conflict between my two names. A convenient coincidence . . . In any case, I make no distinction between Adonis and Ali. My mother calls me Ali . . . I'm very fond of that name, it's the one under which my self came into being; Adonis is the name that introduced me into the cultural sphere.

Adonis has a rather pagan connotation, hasn't it, whereas Ali is strongly associated with monotheism . . .

I am on the side of paganism. But as soon as I sense the least contradiction between the two names, I pull it all back to the beginning, to 'El'.

All the same, hasn't Adonis led Ali a bit too far? Farther than Ali had bargained for?

Adonis is the prolongation of 'El'. The name is different, the image and pronunciation are different, but the essence remains the same . . .

But the contradiction is not confined to the name, it affects the essence too . . .

I don't feel any contradiction.

Are you really the same person, the same as before?

Well, now, that's another question! That person has nothing to do with his name. I am he who was once in the village, and at the same time I am another. I am he who was brought up in the country, for without him I would not be the man I've become. That person, then, is still me, but a 'me' that does not define me in the here and now, a 'me' that has ceased to define me. The 'me'

I am today is the one that defines me. As though some-one were walking along in a body that was always changing, while his mind was unable to stand back (from that body it was born into) enough to understand the contradictions between what it was and what it would become . . . As I see it, a man never 'is': he becomes. A man is not born in a perfect state, he only becomes himself through the life that he makes. Man's identity is the whole arc of his existence, consisting not only in what lies behind but also in what lies ahead.

The fact that you are now Adonis, with all that he represents – does that oblige you to uphold a certain moral standard?

I'm conscious of bearing a considerable responsibility with regard to a great many issues. I fully assume that responsibility, as much in my poetry as in my public stances or my personal relationships . . .

Have you never felt trapped by your image?

I've listened to the views of others about me, I've made efforts to understand them, but I've always done what I wanted or felt deeply compelled to do. For that reason I haven't allowed myself to be deflected from my course, and have avoided the traps set by both praise and censure . . . I've often listened to both ver-sions at once while sticking to the path that seemed to me to be closest to my convictions, to my innermost truth.

That can't be easy.

It certainly is not! You write a thing and some readers say it's no good, while others proclaim that it's brilliant . . . Unless you possess a solid knowledge of yourself and your abilities, you're lost . . .

Self-knowledge is essential because, when all is said and done, nobody in the world can possibly understand us as well as we understand ourselves. Of course, there are many people who only have a careless or imperfect knowledge of themselves, and that's no doubt because their condition, the context in which they live, is not suitable to foster the necessary introspection or to encourage a painstaking exploration of their personal universe.

As for my poetry, I can tell you that nobody understands it as well as I do and, therefore, nobody is better placed to criticize it than I am. After fifty years of writing, I can say that my poetry is still waiting to be read with the proper discernment.

Rather a good sign, I would have thought?

[LATER . . .]

Let's get back to Adonis. Why did you need to adopt that pseudonym? Beyond the story you always tell, about the journals that never published your poems, or slated them.

I don't know . . .

What were you looking for?

Nothing, I hit on it by chance, it wasn't on purpose . . .

But there's no such thing as chance.

I didn't plan it . . .

Even if you didn't plan it, there's nothing innocent about taking a pseudonym, let alone that one. It's as though you wanted to hide behind something. As though you were looking for an alibi. Were you seeking to hide behind this pagan mythological figure in order to make yourself somehow impregnable?

The only explanation for that choice lies, I think, in the issue of exile. It was a name that symbolized my profound sense of being in exile . . .

Even so, a pseudonym establishes a distance between who one truly is and who one wants to become. It also keeps the people around one at arm's length. It sometimes allows us to fabricate a 'character' to hide behind . . . I'm thinking of my two 'idols', Marilyn and Bowie. Marilyn Monroe constructed a persona for herself behind which she was both concealed and revealed. Then she couldn't shake it off, until in the end she was defeated by it . . . And David Bowie, he cast himself as several characters (Ziggy Stardust, Aladdin Sane, the Thin White Duke) and almost came a cropper . . . The danger is that the character takes over, so you don't know who you are any more. Did you never feel you were losing control?

No, never.

What did you gain by choosing that pseudonym? What did Adonis bring to you, and what did it take away?

It annoyed a lot of people . . .

No, I'm talking about you. What did Adonis do for you? Explain it to me properly: why did you choose that pseudonym? What did it represent for you?

It was a coincidence, I wasn't thinking consciously —

So if it was just a coincidence, why did you keep it?

Because as soon as I started using it, it worked. People began to identify me with the name Adonis.

Which one rubbed off onto the other most, Ali or Adonis?

Adonis, of course! If I want to go unnoticed these days, I sign as Ali. Ali has become a mere name on a passport, an administrative name . . .

[ANOTHER DAY . . .]

How do you suppose people will regard you after your death? Do you ever think about that?

Absolutely not.

Do you never project yourself imaginatively into the future in that way?

No, I don't, it holds no interest for me. And besides, it's impossible to control the image other people cultivate of one. All that I care about is that people should understand me. The only thing I wish for is to be considered objectively.

Not long ago, I was out with some friends who were talking about you. I was completely gobsmacked at the way one of them was going on! You'd have thought he was invoking the sayings and doings of some legendary or popular hero, whom no one had actually met . . . This man's demeanour, his whole narrative style, reminded me of traditional story-tellers in the old coffee houses of Damascus!

What was he saying?

I was struck first of all by his posture. He was sitting on a couch, facing me. He wriggled up to the edge of the couch where he took up this rather stiff, straight position, back and pelvis supporting the weight of his body. His legs were spread. The right side angled forward, he was braced on his right foot, the left slightly bent back . . . His eyes shone and he conducted the cadences of his story with rhythmic gestures. I sank back into my seat, watching the show attentively. So he says: 'Do you know what Adonis likes best of all about a house?' Everyone else had eager smiles on their faces, look-ing faintly embarrassed and yet clearly recognizing the importance of the question. 'No, what does he like?' And this man bursts out: 'The bathroom! That's the most important room for him . . . It provides a wholesome start to his day!' To which everyone choruses (even me, I got quite carried away): 'Is that so?! How amazing! How right he is!' I was stunned and yet at the same time I felt I couldn't say any-

thing. That's when I realized what a celebrity you really are. If it's like that now, it'll be a frenzy when you're gone! Everyone with their pet story to tell!

You can't control that kind of thing. What are you going to do? Nothing . . .

Well yes, it's true, there's nothing to be done . . .

It just shows people's mentality . . .

I know, but he was talking about you as if you were dead, as if this was a definitive truth that couldn't be disputed by anyone! I was shocked! What does it make you think?

Nothing.

All right, but it happened in front of me, I found myself in the position of being both witness and hostage at once . . .

But it's only a minority!

The person who told that story was not criticizing you, no — he was a perfectly sweet, young man. What shocks me is the way you've been made into a feature of other people's lives and conversation . . . As though they had some kind of power over you.

Well, the fact is people tell all sorts of stories about me. I've heard it said that I own palatial homes here there and everywhere, in New York, Japan, Paris and London!

[LATER . . .]

How do you relate to your looks? Were you aware early on of being such a handsome and attractive man?

No, I only realized that recently — too late!

Oh, sure! (Laughter.) You can't think I'll fall for that one!

No, it's true, it only came home to me recently, a few years ago!

Can't believe it . . . (Laughter.)

I'm afraid it's somewhat pitiful from my point of view! To have such potential as a heart-throb and never to have known it! (*Laughter.*)

Incredible.

I only woke up to these virtues of mine twenty years ago. Or let's say perhaps a little earlier, when I reached forty . . .

Well, I've seen pictures of you at forty, and you were a total bombshell, atomic, no less! Are you seriously telling me that when you were twenty you had no idea?

None whatsoever. I've often told the story of how girls always liked me and I couldn't think why! I paid them no attention at all, I was far too busy with the construction of my identity and my culture . . . And also I was so poor, I simply didn't have the means.

It's not a question of means, it's more about self-awareness . . .

I didn't feel any need to go out with women, I lacked the obsession, it never occurred to me . . . The only way to explain it is by the fact that I was simply too caught up in the construction of my self and my world . . . I was preoccupied by my own problems as well. I couldn't afford to ask a girl out for a drink or a meal, I was very poor, scarcely able to keep body and soul together . . .

As a result, I only discovered my success with women when it was too late! (*Laughter.*) Some of them are actually much younger—I expect they see their father in me. I say to them: 'But I'm old enough to be your father!' Cries of protest from the girls: 'You, a poet, and you're bothered about age?!' (*Laughter.*)

And I say to them: 'But it's a fact!' In any case, I've never had the time to spare for that kind of fling. As one grows older, time is increasingly the only capital one has left. The time that remains to me is intensely precious. I have to make the most out of every hour that passes, for my work, or in doing something constructive. Otherwise I have the impression that it is wasted . . .

To go back to this business of attractiveness. How did you deal with it? It's always a problem being dishy and charming, let alone, as in your case, a poet and an intellectual as well . . . Is it difficult to handle? Is it not a bit of an ordeal?

It's never worried me.

It only turns into a pressure once you're aware of it, you mean?

When you find out that you are handsome, desirable, eligible and chased after, it can well become a headache and lead to complications in your dealings with others. But I never had that problem. There's probably a further reason for this: I've never believed that the solution to my problems lay in the domain of love or romance. If there is a solution, as far as I'm concerned it can only be found in the domain of writing and poetry . . . If I had to choose between writing and having an affair with a very beautiful woman, I would choose writing without a moment's hesitation. Not that I consider poetry to be superior to the experience with a woman. Woman *is* poetry, living poetry . . . And yet, to me, nothing expresses my existence better than to create . . .

What about your body? Do you feel free with your body?

Yes, I like my body very much, and I take care of it. But my 'love for my body' was another late development. I've always felt free about my body. But freedom only thrives in certain conditions. I've never confused freedom with the debasement of that freedom. I've known a lot of people whose notion of freedom had become warped, leading them to treat their bodies with disrespect. I have always respected and looked after my body, but when I give it, I give it completely . . . It's not so badly preserved, considering my age! (*Laughter.*) My friends or brothers are surprised when they see me . . .

*Could you explain what you mean by 'debasing the body'?
Am I debasing my body if I make love to more than one person? Without falling into the cliché of 'make love not war',[1]
I think that if you know how to choose your partners, having numerous sexual encounters can be very enriching and
can teach you to know your body more intimately. It's
another way of communicating with a person, of getting to
know them . . . A fulfilling sex-life is rather like creativity –
it makes us feel we exist, and reminds us that we possess a
living body with desires and pleasures of its own . . . I'm not
saying that sexuality is enough by itself – that would be terribly boring. But I could never accuse anyone, male or
female, of abusing their bodies just because they were
involved with more than one sexual partner! Another thing
is that there's a double standard for men and women in this
area. A woman is often labelled a 'tart' if she has several partners and lovers. On the other hand, a man in the same situation is admired as a playboy, a stud, a hero! To my mind that's
completely unacceptable. Love is a part of life. Making love is
one of the ways to celebrate life, celebrate our bodies . . .*

*While we're on the subject, let me tell you a little story
that shows that love and the body aren't taboo in Muslim
countries only. In 1998 I was in New York with Samer. We
were deeply in love, and Samer had just finished his degree
at Columbia University. He was showing me around the
city. We were strolling hand in hand and every now and
then, in a surge of emotion and desire, we'd hug and kiss as
lovers do, as they do all over the world, or at least in some*

47

parts of the world . . . Because there, to my astonishment, in Manhattan, New York, USA, the home of individual freedoms, cars kept slowing down beside us and their drivers yelling aggressively: 'Hey! Go do that somewhere else!' or 'You're disgusting, there are places for that kind of muck!'

If I spoke of debasement, it's because I regard the human body as the most beautiful thing there is. Once cheapened, it becomes the same as any other object, shorn of its specificity, a common and commonplace object. The body is unique and this uniqueness is to be cherished. Having said that, I agree that, sexually speaking, a body needs other bodies. But always in a framework of mutual respect, friendship and love . . . The flesh belongs to nature, it's on the side of animality . . . but an animality that can rise above nature, and thus attain freedom. And freedom is not a trivial matter. It's a responsibility.

Have women played an important role in your life?

Very much so. Life would be meaningless without women. The effect of women upon my life has been both positive and negative . . . To be honest, I learned most from the negative aspects. I learned that love, or whatever it is we call by that name, can never provide an answer to the real problems we face. For me, there's no such thing as love without a sound basis in friendship. If you can't tell to your husband or wife the things you tell to your best friend, then you don't love them. Every great love must be founded upon a great friendship. I've also known lies; I have come to suspect that lying is an intrinsic part of our love lives. How does falsehood enter into a caring relationship? It's a question that often disturbs me. If love were grounded in friendship, surely there'd be no more need to lie . . .

Yes, but nobody lies just for the fun of it . . .

It's a means of self-defence.

No, it's a way of protecting—

It's unworthy of a person in love. Two lovers, spending a lifetime together, why do they lie to each other? It brings up some uncomfortable questions . . . There must be a dysfunction somewhere . . .

Personally I don't believe in confiding every single thing—some things are best kept to oneself and not shared with one's partner in love.

Telling the other person the truth can be like 'selling one's soul', because truth, or 'purity of feeling', doesn't exist.

To insist on complete openness and sincerity, the whole truth and nothing but the truth, is a form of enslavement . . . It's a way of boxing the other person in, placing them under an eternal threat of recrimination. To demand the truth is to stand over them like a judge, an authority who can tot up the evidence in this way or that. For who's to say how the other will react to this 'confession' of truth? And if he feels wounded by it, he can always pretend to say truthfully, 'I understand', or, worse still, 'I forgive you'. I am all for respecting one's spouse, but that doesn't imply telling the truth non-stop. We have to allow ourselves a margin of survival or self-determination . . .

I find it oppressive to always tell the truth. There are things I'd rather keep private, that I don't feel like sharing, not even with the man I live with. I believe in independence within couplehood. If purity and truth are what you're after, you'd be better off finding religion and marrying God! No danger of being let down there! His perfection is unverifiable, after all . . . Me, I prefer 'flawed' men. So-called perfect people bore me.

Having said that, I do believe in absolute love, with all its failings and ups and downs . . . a love that's stronger than all else, stronger than death, stronger than children, stronger than life . . . It's an adolescent fantasy, I know, but I believe and want to go on believing forever in the possibility of crazy, mad love, overcoming all sorts of obstacles. I'm not afraid of that.

But if two lovers are lying to each other, why do they stay together? Let them go their separate ways. I say that he who lies in mind, lies in body also. Falsehood deforms everything, including the physical side. Sex becomes reduced to a mechanical transaction . . .

Two people may stay together for all sorts of reasons. I consider lying to be a part of life, so I must take that into account and, on occasion, submit to it. As for the 'lying body', it may be that men are more sensitive on this point than women are

. . . Men have more reason to wonder whether their partner genuinely feels pleasure with them! (Laughter.)

But my original question concerned the role of women in your life, not simply on the sexual or emotional level, but in general.

I don't think it's easy for a man and a woman to be friends. If friendship blossoms between them, it may turn into love, but can love ever turn back into friendship? I know a couple who were once in love and then separated, but remained friends. I wonder how they did it. It seems very odd to me . . . If there is a firm, deep friendship uniting a man and a woman, and their relationship ends, then as far as I'm concerned it's all over.

I agree.

To return to what we were saying about lies . . . I think you're right, sometimes it is necessary to lie, because to come face to face with truth is like coming face to face with death. Absolute truth is a kind of death.

Do you think that a man can spend his whole life with one woman? Are human beings monogamous?

No, I think a body needs many bodies.

Of course, because man is naturally polygamous.

Man?

The human race . . .

It's something that needs stating more often.

Perhaps in fifty or a hundred years! Meanwhile, we're going through a period of transition. It'll be a long time before our nature ceases to be taboo. We all know we need several partners over the course of a lifetime, yet there are so many moral or religious barriers against it – especially for women . . . One keeps coming up against that imbalance.

At the stage we're at, it seems that people find it hard to admit their polygamy. Everyone claims to be searching for the 'ideal man' or the 'ideal woman'.

And that's why I say that lying is such a deplorable thing.

I think adultery is part of marriage, or couplehood. If you get married, you should take that on board, and face the likelihood of your partner's infidelity. That's the reason I'm not married. I can't stand the idea of spending my whole life with one man! Even if that's my dream deep down, I know it's impossible!

You're liable to pay dearly for that choice . . .

It always happens, whatever you do. Either you love someone and then you fall in love with someone else, or your partner falls in love with someone else . . . It's just what happens. You are assuming that feelings are stable and last a lifetime. Even without infidelity, there are couples who stop caring about each other after a few years of marriage . . . Can one ever love a person with the same intensity to the end?

So what's the answer?

Either you have to get divorced every time you cheat on some-one or fall out of love with them, and get remarried; or else you carry on sharing your lives even though you're not in love any more, and follow parallel paths, each one for him or herself but staying married. There's no third solution. It's awful, but that's how I see it. I know how painful it is to break up, it's like a bereavement, like being ripped in two, and it shatters your self-confidence . . . You just want to die, to take revenge . . . I've been through the mill that way, and the grief is just as great, even for a teenager. Or it can even be worse, because at that age you're still naïve enough to idealize love and the beloved. If you buy into the idea of marriage and you get married, then you have to accept its terms and limitations.

I would get rid of the whole institution . . .

You would?

It should simply be abolished.

We're forgetting one thing, which is that we live in Europe, where it's okay to live with someone without being married. One can even have children without being married. But in a country where women have no status at all unless they are virgins, or wives and mothers (and even then they might not have any rights, as in Arab-Muslim countries), well, there you've got no choice except to get married, and you can't even opt for a civil ceremony!

Isn't cohabitation now beginning to be practised all the same?

Fortunately it is, but, if people want children, they have to tie the knot. Otherwise their offspring won't have any legal existence or rights.

2 Mut'a, a contract between a man and a woman which pays an agreed sum to the woman in exchange for sexual relations. This form of union is only permitted for certain Shia Muslims.

But you can contract a 'temporary marriage',[2] like the Shia . . .

Only if you're a Shia.

Yes, or if you symbolically become one for the sake of appearances. At any rate the formula exists.

I know, but it's still within a religious framework!

True . . . but it goes beyond religion . . .

Speaking of women, you've always claimed to prefer them in their 'natural' state. No lipstick, no makeup, no perfume, nothing. I've never understood that preference. Are you scared of sophisticated women? I think it's wonderful that women can decide whether to make themselves up or not, decide whether they feel like stepping out in fishnet stockings, high-heeled shoes and backless dresses, or plain old jeans and trainers. I love it when women decorate their bodies with makeup, tattoos or piercings . . .

Would you be attracted to a man who wore makeup?

But I'm talking about women . . . All right then, I find that men look great with some kohl around the eyes! And earrings are lovely and sexy on men . . .

A woman's skin is a beautiful thing, which should be allowed to breathe and live. Why hide it under something so much less interesting?

Let's be serious, and make a distinction. If you want to make love to a woman whose skin is all sticky with foundation or mascara and whose hair is all plastered with gel, I'll grant you, it's not much of a turn-on! (Laughter.) I was asking you about women in a different context, not a sexual situation.

I can understand a woman with wonderful eyes adding something to highlight them, so long as the makeup doesn't swamp the face.

Well, I'm all for artifice. I think it's important.

I don't like it myself.

Why not?

It's a matter of taste. I have nothing against lipstick, only it must be in harmony with the face . . . I can understand the allure of 'artifice', I'm not against it, but I personally don't like it. I prefer women to be unmade-up, no doubt because I find skin to be a most erotic site of contact with the outside world. I can't imagine a barrier between our skin and the world.

Seduction is precisely that, a means of communicating with the world.

I say to the woman I love, 'To me you look lovely as you are, without makeup . . . So who are you painting your face for? If it's for me, don't bother!'

But it's for herself! If she likes herself with lipstick on, what are you going to do?

Nothing, I don't say a word, I put up with it.

Really?

I was only telling you my preference . . .

So you're not dead set against women who wear makeup?

No, no, not at all.

Among all the various sorts who disapprove of women wearing makeup, there are the hard-line feminists, who think of themselves as blokes . . . And traditionalist, bigoted men, of course, who think a woman has to be 'pure' and 'natural', seeing as she is impure 'by nature' and must be kept away from any artificiality that might enhance her charms. But as soon as she becomes a mother, her status changes, and then she might be permitted a liberty or two!

[ANOTHER DAY . . .]

There is a great tradition of erotic writing in Arab culture. The texts are nothing special from a stylistic point of view, as they were written in simplified, everyday language; their content, on the other hand, is amazingly arousing! The ones I've read date from the tenth to the eighteenth or nineteenth centuries. What do these writings stand for in Arab culture? What did they contribute to society? What place did they occupy, what influence did they exert up to our own times?

There are a great number of erotic texts in the annals of Arab poetry. The ones you refer to have been absorbed into popular culture. They are not a part of high culture, for a variety of religious, moral and linguistic reasons. All the same, they were read in secret by many people whose erotic and sexual culture was entirely shaped by those books. That's how it was in the past. Nowadays, erotic literature is two-a-penny, anybody can get hold of it, especially with today's media . . . I think those books are very significant, and the curious thing is that the majority of the authors were theologians and clerics. It says a good deal for their open-mindedness and loving gaze upon life. I value those texts enormously, but they played no part in cultural life . . .

How strange. And what a shame!

It's because of religion, the moral pressure it brings to bear.

What intrigues me is that this rich, erotic literature exists, focused on the body and carnal pleasures, all about men loving women, women loving men, men loving men, women loving women, and there's also a great vein of learned erotic

3 Theory of libertinism.

4 Omar Bin Abi Rabiaa (644–712): Arab poet famed for his amatory verses.

poetry (Ibahiyya[3]) in the work of Omar Bin Abi Rabiaa[4] and others. What's left of all that? Why, given this cultural inheritance, are Arab societies still so conservative? Why is the body still taboo today, or rather, today more than ever before? . . . Why the constant straining towards transcendence? They fantasize, they dream, they hope, but everything remains in the head, as if it were beyond them to act. Is it an effect of oral culture? The word mattering more than the deed? You can talk, but you can't do? Perhaps the Arabs are afraid of their overdeveloped 'erotic charge'. So they hide it, they mask it, by practising 'psychological ablations' in a haze of Surahs and rituals . . . (Not to speak of the harem, which did its bit to 'eroticize' the Arab-Muslim world. Occidental fantasies wallowed in the availability of harem women offered up like objects, like slaves, whose own desires were irrelevant.) Are dreams and fantasies the best way to escape from an everyday reality bogged down in tradition and the constraints of religion?

Your last hypothesis is the most plausible, I'd say. Religion weighs heavy on the individual. That is why Arab societies came up with the idea of a life on two levels: one secret and private, in which everyone gives in to lust and all sorts of sensual pleasures—and no other people has taken pleasure to greater heights, to my knowledge!—and another, official level that's strictly observant. If you read Arab history, it's packed with intense dramas played out between men and women. Men who die for love of a woman, or pursue her through foreign lands, or murder the husband in order to possess her, or simply abduct her . . . These men allowed themselves complete licence, but they did so in secret, behind closed doors, to avoid any conflict with religion and society at large. For the public face of Arab societies was a pious, conservative one, respectful of tradition and the Koranic texts . . . Even today, Arab society runs on these parallel tracks. One hidden and permissive, the other ostentatiously religious. It could be argued that the Arab personality is equally two-faced, being founded on lies and hypocrisy. Can we stop now?

Have you had enough?

It's nine o'clock. We've made good progress, haven't we?

We've done one chapter.

Oh well, that's plenty!

Are you tired?

No, do you want to go on?

If you're up to it, yes . . .

Part Two?

Yes.

How many parts are there?

Ten.

(!)

I've got roughly one hundred questions.

So we've done about a quarter?

Not quite that much but since you're warmed up and in full flow — let's press on, into the heart of the matter . . .

On we go, then!

My Heart Belongs to Daddy
(MARILYN MONROE, 1960)

NINAR: *How would you define fatherhood? Because person-ally I don't know very much about how fathers behave with daughters, or with children generally. In the Arab East, a father is someone who brings home the money and basically says 'No'. I exaggerate, of course, I caricature, I stereotype! The father is a figure of substance, especially outside the home. What kind of a father were you with me? Would you have been different if you hadn't lost your own father when you were twenty-one?*

ADONIS: In all societies, and especially Arab societies, the father is an absolute master; he's the one who gives the orders and expects them to be obeyed. He seeks to rear his children in his own image, so as to pass on his values and moral standards to them. That's why such societies are thought of as patriarchal. Once upon a time matriarchal societies existed, but these have died out, regrettably . . .

The father in Arab culture is a scaled-down image of God Almighty, an absolute authority who must never be challenged. As a result Arab fathers tend to treat their children as putty, raw material, to be moulded into whatever shape they please. There are countless studies and reports that condemn these societies for stifling their children, for not allowing them the chance to exist in their own right. And these same children are condemned to repeat the pattern with their own offspring . . .

You should take a look at Hisham Sharabi's work, which has analysed this phenomenon in depth.

As a father myself, I never attempted to play that game. But it turned out that my children were the ones who couldn't accept it, or didn't understand it! I wanted you girls to grow up without interference from me. I suppose that left its mark. It may even have damaged you, because old habits of human interaction were already embedded. Neither of you wanted the traditional father–daughter relationship, and yet there was a vaccum of authority around you.

You grew up in a climate that failed to provide certain things. This had a repercussion on your characters and conduct.

I thought your mother could make up for the lack, but she couldn't . . . Actually, I'm glad you're conscious of all this. I think to myself that, with other children and other parents, things could easily have turned out worse.

All the same, I feel it was wrong of me not to have exercised any parental authority at all. I misread the situation . . . I relied on your mother to take care of that side of things. But that was clearly a mistake. If only I could go back and start again, but I can't . . .

I rather like the idea of letting children grow up without a father-figure. Of course, it depends on the society. In Europe, where there are more and more one-parent families, things are easier on the kids, since there's not just one model of family but several, from childless couples who adopt to gay couples who live together with one or the other's children . . . But in Lebanon, when we were small, it was tough for us on many fronts. There was a more violent kind of insecurity. We were at war. And yet maybe that's what saved us . . . The war was a source of anguish, but at the same time it made horror and fear almost routine . . . We had to survive everything at once. It was permanent chaos, terror looming from all sides . . . So we had to bring out the big guns, so to speak! We just had to adapt, and set up mechanisms of self-defence that would help us to resist. Except that these mechanisms, once installed, tend to dig themselves in, and when you start living a normal life — in France for example — you keep coming up against the old defences . . . Like too-small shoes, or tight corsets that hurt . . . You have to remove them, without fearing the sudden absence of pain.

Perhaps what made things even harder and more intractable was that your mother never said a word to me about you. She knew everything about your problems, your blunders, but she never mentioned them, as though I'd been a stranger. I had disqualified myself as a father, I suppose . . .

But I want you to know that the reason she didn't tell you is because we asked her not to. At least, I always asked her not to tell you anything.

I don't know the exact reasons, I'm just telling you how it was. The fact is that your mother never came to me and said, 'Arward or Ninar is having this or that problem.' I know I'm to blame for a serious error of judgement, but this lack of communication only made matters worse.

I wouldn't know, that's between you and Mum! She was always running after me with 'Your father this, your father that', 'Go and see your father', 'Did you say hello to your father?' 'Did you give him his kiss?' 'Have you shown him your drawing?' It drove me round the bend! It was so maddening that I'd refuse point-blank, or comply with gritted teeth. I'd go, 'I'm fed up with it, stop nagging me about him!' (Laughter.)

How unlike her, she never told me! (*Laughter.*)

It used to annoy me no end. Oh, the rows we had about it! I used to call her 'the counsel for the defence'!

[A FEW MINUTES LATER . . .]

Do you think people should make up different fatherhoods, tailored to the children they've got?

No one can invent their own fatherhood, what one does is to create a behaviour. I think it's high time one challenges the image and behaviour of the father in Arab societies.

I was only trying to find out whether you had a different way of being when you were with Arwad or me. What did you invent with me? And with Arwad?

Hard to say, because I was so little at home, working to make ends meet. My absences and trips were very bad for your education. I   hardly ever saw you . . .

Well, if one's not physically around, one can't do anything . . . That's why I'm asking — can there be several sorts of fatherhood?

How do you mean, several fatherhoods?

Several ways of doing things.

Several sorts of fatherhood? Yes, of course.

On the father's initiative, or the children's?

That would obviously depend on the father's behaviour and mentality. Every father is different.

How were you affected by your father's early death? What were the repercussions of that for you?

I was very lucky at the time. Circumstances obliged me to work extremely hard to make a name for myself and to get ahead; as a result, I wasn't so handicapped by the death of my father.

Were there pressures that you sought out, that you created, in order to distract yourself from your father's death? To fill the void?

No, I had to, I had to work in order to send my brother Hussein to school, and my sister Fatima. My father's death did change me in that I was suddenly forced to come to grips with the practical side of life. I realized that without financial independence, I'd never make it . . . I learned to be careful of the material aspects of life, and how to administer them. I had to work hard, there was no one but myself to support the family . . .

Do you think you might have reproduced the model of the absent father in your own life?

Possibly. Especially as my father didn't really bring me up but left me to find my own way.

[SOME TIME LATER . . .]

Are you at all surprised, or put out, by the fact that I don't read your work?

Not in the least.

And why do you think I don't?

It's not something that saddens me. On the contrary, it's crossed my mind that you ought not to read me — the better to create your own personality as freely as possible. Far better than being influenced by me.

It makes me even happier to see that whilst you don't, as you say, read my work, you're producing something all your own, something different. I would be upset, though, if you both didn't read me and didn't produce anything fresh . . .

*People often ask me, 'What did you learn from your father?'
'How has he influenced you?' 'What traits of his have come
down to you?' I hate those questions, and yet whenever I try
to answer them I don't know what to say. I cast about and
can only answer mechanically, like: 'Respect for others; self-
criticism; dislike of ostentation.' What do you think – what
have you passed down to me?*

Tolerance, certainly . . . I don't know, perhaps stubborn-
ness as well, perseverance . . . Even if you haven't actually accomplished anything so far! (*Laughter.*)

A love for others, perhaps . . . Refusal to resort to
violence, respect for human beings. Refusal to be sub-
missive. A belief in yourself.

*It must be disturbing to recognize your own features in the
faces of your daughters. More than in the face of a son, or
not? Like seeing yourself cross-dressed as a girl? I can't tell,
I haven't got kids yet (only a pair of cats!) but I'm sure I'd
find it unsettling . . .*

I rather like it.

Isn't it a sort of transvestite feeling?

There's something lacking in a man with no feminine
traits, I think. Likewise, in a woman with no masculine
traits. I can only be delighted when I get a glimpse of
my daughters' masculine side . . .

I was talking about features, your features . . .

Yes, of my character . . .

No, not your character. You physically.

When I note that your eyes are like mine, I feel pleased.

That's all? Isn't it disturbing to see yourself in female form?

No, it allows me to see the feminine part in myself.

And it's not at all disturbing?

Not to me, no.

A mini-copy of oneself?

There's no such thing as a copy in this context . . .

I know that. I only ask because I'm thirty-three and child-less. I don't want to have kids . . . I don't want to give birth to a being who's going to die!

I adore my two cats, but I don't see myself in them, even if I sometimes think we're getting to be fearfully alike!

This aspect of having a child intrigues me a lot. If, say, I had a little boy one day, I might well feel a bit shaken to see my features reproduced in him.

[LATER . . .]

Do you think it's important to pass things on to one's children?

No, I don't.

You don't?!

No, since theoretically I'd want my children to be the opposite of me, excelling in whatever they do. I couldn't care less whether they were like me or not.

And you're not out to transmit certain values to them?

No, nor do I impose anything on them. All that matters to me is that they should be brilliant at their work, at whatever they do for a trade. Whatever that happens to be.

Might the business of transmitting things to one's children have something to do with eternity? If you continue to exist through me, for instance, and I in turn pass down what you taught me, well, you won't be around to appreciate it . . . I see no point in having children just so that a part of us can live on posthumously. What good is that to me — I won't be here to see it! And children, for their part, have better things to do than to take their place in some lineage . . . It's all so self-deluding, it makes me despair. But there you are, most people do have children, often without really wanting them, thoughtlessly, by force of custom . . .

What matters is to pass on ideas, rather than a physical resemblance.

I quite agree, but there are lots of people who have children purely for the sake of it!

Yes, because they have nothing else to do, or they have nothing else, full stop. They imagine they're going to last for ever through their physiognomy. In my village, when someone's child came out looking exactly like him, they'd say: 'He's been spat out by his father'!

Yes, they imagine themselves living on through their children . . .

People have their weak spots . . .

But then what's the point of having children?

Basically, it's in order to reproduce the human race. If everyone thought as you do, there wouldn't be any-body left to people the future!

But there are six and a half billion of us already!

If those six billion thought like you, pretty soon there would be no more children at all!

You mean, people make babies for economic reasons?

For the sake of survival, for our continuation . . .

Continuation? What's the use of that? The Earth itself is going to perish one day, and so is the Sun!

That's a separate problem entirely, nothing to do with preserving the species.

All right, but why this obsession with preserving the species?

Would you rather humans became extinct?

You bet I would! (Laughter.)

Ah, then you should have said so straightaway! (*Laughter.*)

No, but seriously, I want to know the reason why.

Because the human kind is the most beautiful species alive.

Yes . . .

There's nothing more beautiful. It must be protected.

So why don't they start by protecting the specimens who are alive on earth right now? The people who are dying from star-vation, diseases, wars . . . Of course mankind has got to be protected, but there's plenty to be getting along with.

Coming back to the subject of children: do you know I didn't want to have any? You two arrived by mistake!

Yes, I know.

You knew that? You both knew, you and Arward? Your mother and I barely had enough money to buy food, or to live on . . . We weren't about to have children and force them to suffer hardship with us! And then when you arrived, you were just splendid! (*Laughter.*)

Yes, that's always the way, I gather.

Just splendid, you were . . . Let's see, now, since you came along by mistake, would you have preferred not to come along at all? (*Laughter.*)

It's a bit late now!

Come on, as a matter of principle, do you wish you'd never set eyes on this world?

I do, sometimes.

Sometimes, fair enough. But in principle?

I don't care much either way. To be honest, I don't know . . . Having had no say in the decision, I can't answer your question.

No one's ever had a say . . .

At times I feel that life is no big deal.

Really? You're not afraid of death?

Oh, I am, I'm petrified . . .

So why can't you say that life is a great thing?

Because I've grown accustomed to being alive, not because it's so great.

You can't mean that!

Tell me what's so great about it.

So why do you live, then?

I don't know—I was put here, I have to do something or die of boredom. That's it.

That can be enough. Therefore, you have to make something of your life.

I've reached a point where I can say that I live for my artistic work and to be with my friends, enjoying and sharing with them. Once I realized that I couldn't run away any more, that I had to go on existing, I decided to throw open the sluices and let everything inside me pour out. I jumped in with my head down, not knowing where I was going, letting my own current pull me along . . . I've found my reason for living. I live for my creative work, for the world I bring into being. And anything that gets in my way, I chuck it out. Work is the only thing that keeps me going. But without my work I don't know what I'd do, because life seems to

me extremely violent, and death reigns with absolute com-
mand over all.

But life can be the most beautiful thing. A desirable woman, a desirable man, whom you love . . .

Oh yes, but all that's so transitory.

Life gives you the chance to create, so you have a sense of making the world, of giving it a brand-new image.

Now, yes, since I've been dedicating all my time and energy to my work. Still, you have to remember, my wartime experience left me a little paranoid and cut off from reality.

It was a period in your life. There were millions of girls like you.

Each person undergoes an experience in her own way, and, what's more important, to the best of her ability. Just because there are X million girls who sailed through the war and came out unscathed doesn't mean that I will, necessarily.

That's true, but these are cases that are repeated throughout history, and whatever is historical is therefore not ontological.

Ontological?

It doesn't actually put existence at stake. Anything that is historical, man can overcome and go beyond.

It's true that you might be able to overcome it, but it leaves a mark, it scars you . . . Don't forget how little I was!

Yes, but man is powerful, there's nothing he can't do.

[LATER . . .]

I wonder if two people can love each other without having children?

Of course.

And can they stay together without children?

Oh, without children their chances of staying together are positively improved. Because when a child comes to a couple, it turns everything upside down. Its presence configures a new pattern, a new dynamic . . . Children are like a small revolution inside the house.

Inside the couple.

Yes.

So why do people have them, knowing that their arrival will be like an earthquake for the relationship?

There are various reasons why people have children, and not all of them are interesting . . .

Do you wish you'd had a boy? A little Ali? A future Adonis, perhaps?

I've never framed it in those terms, never thought about it, quite simply because I've never seen the difference between having a boy or a girl.

Lemon Inceste

(SERGE AND CHARLOTTE GAINSBOURG, 1984)

NINAR: *Although I don't read your work, do you think I might be able to sense or pick up something of your poetry even so? Is your poetry a condition of the soul? A contagious disease?*

ADONIS: I should be asking you that question! It's directed at you, not me! (*Laughter.*)

Oh dear, you're right!

Your good health! (*Sound of wineglasses clinking.*) Does that question start off a new section?

Yes.

Then let's stop.

Are you sure? Let me press you further.[1]

But it's half past nine!

I know. Let's just go on till ten o'clock! (Laughter.)

1 Translation from the Arabic: *Khallini e'sorak shuway ba'ed*!

79

Now, concentration please . . . I have no perception of your poetry as a direct experience. On the other hand, I can perceive that you are a rare person, who has his own world, and a way of being that is very special: great rigour in your work plus extreme sensibility . . . All that I can sense.

That might be enough, don't you think?

What I can't get at is the poetry itself, as a text, as a structure . . . Except for the beat, perhaps. I think I can feel the beat. It must be like you. It must reflect the rhythms your body has, your body in daily life when you're walking about, when you get impatient, when you're eating, when you're laughing . . . And especially when you're making love. Well, I wouldn't know about that! (Laughter.) *And yet I feel sure your poetry is wired to the most intimate rhythms of your body, to its pleasures and raptures and sorrows . . . But that side is none of my business!*

[LATER . . .]

What do you think about traditional fathers who choose their daughters' husbands (often, in fact, from amongst their own friends); do you think they project themselves into them? Or have I got a hopelessly twisted mind? But try as I might, I can't understand it!

It's all rather psychological, a bit Freudian. I don't know . . . It depends on the father. All I can say is, I'm not convinced by Freud. At least not on that point.

Really!

I'm not convinced by psychoanalysis in general, I think it's hopelessly compromised by errors and over-statements. Attempting to analyse something as complex and many-sided as a human being, with the focus narrowed onto one single aspect—it's too arbitrary, too contrived. A person, whoever he may be, is always a mixture, a vast combination of feelings, emotions and dreams. The notion of boiling him down, pouring him into a vessel and declaring 'behold the result' is both violent and restrictive. I am against this way of looking at things.

What about Lacan?

Lacan is the prolongation of Freud. It was he who led what he called the 'return to Freud', after all. You can't analyse human nature with sole reference to Freud—it's an appalling reduction. Human beings are so complex! In spite of this, some psychoanalyses prove effective and can be undeniably helpful. There are people who may need an interlocutor from time to time, someone who will listen to them, in a reassuring atmosphere; but that won't cure them.

You're not cured by the analyst, you cure yourself.

But what if the person has a friend he trusts completely—couldn't he talk to him?

It's not the same. It's not the same thing at all. A friend can't be 'objective', or keep a detached perspective on things

. . .

No, but he's close?

No way! Friends aren't objective. They'll start offering advice or making comments that reflect their own attitudes and prejudices. Whereas the psychoanalyst is trained to establish a distance from the patient. He won't give advice, he won't pass judgement on religious or moral grounds. Suppose you're reluctant to have children, or you're gay. Your friend is bound to make some idiotic remark, like: 'Every normal person dotes on children' or 'Homosexuality is a sin' ... You might be feeling lonely and desperate. When someone says that kind of thing it can make you feel even more isolated, you could break down ... It could drive some people to kill themselves!

I think the psychoanalyst's job is to steer clear of religious or moral issues while at the same time keeping the patient in touch with reality, without judging him ... And so you learn to accept yourself, and face your weaknesses. You accomplish this entirely by yourself.

I'm talking from experience, but I don't know the first thing about psychoanalytic theory, nor much about Freud. All I know is the bare minimum I learned for my baccalaureate! But let's get back to the topic of fathers who choose their daughters' husbands from among men who come from the same social background, with the same outlook and the same religion – men who even look like them, sometimes! I find that downright suspect, verging on the incestuous ... As if the father, unable to 'go' with her himself, were setting her up with a stand-in. My impression is that these fathers are marrying their daughters by proxy!

Why don't you look at it another way? If the future husband is a family friend, the father will automatically feel reassured about his daughter's safety, about her chances of being treated with respect.

Oh no, that doesn't follow at all. The man can easily be her father's friend or even a member of his family, and turn out to be a rotten husband who doesn't love her or who beats her up.

Indeed, but that's another problem, and nothing to do with incest.

Maybe so, but it shows the father's ignorance. Because being a mate of his doesn't guarantee that the man will make a good son-in-law who loves and respects his daughter!

If he's ignorant, that's another problem. It doesn't alter the fact that he will make that assumption. The girls in my village are always encouraged to marry a cousin — 'better than going with a stranger', as they say. So they all intermarry just to keep things inside the family, and reassure the father as much as possible on his daughters' account.

Pretty fishy, in my opinion.

You may be right.

I often compare other men to you, looking for the 'Adonis' in them. What about you — if you wanted to love a woman, if you were seeking to have an affair, do you think that deep down you'd be looking out for a girl who had something of me? (Smiles.)

(*Blushing, choking and laughing out loud.*) It's possible! It's not unthinkable . . .

How do you mean?

It's possible, but I wouldn't take that as a symptom of incestuous yearnings.

No, but I would.

I'd explain it more in terms of echoes, complementarities; a better chance of a good match. There's also the element of self-love: I love myself and so I'm drawn to a man—or a woman—who looks like me. It's nothing to do with incest.

But one can just as well fall for someone completely unlike oneself. Is it necessary to love a person who looks like one-self? Why be matched on the physical level only?

I only said that about the hypothetical possibility of a woman resembling you.

You'll have to say more . . . (Silence.) *To what extent do you allow yourself to think about me?*

(*Laughter.*) We need to distinguish two levels here. First, I don't think about you, you are in me. Like the air that I breathe, like the sun overhead, you are an important part of my life. Second, when I see this important part of my life being idle, I imagine how brilliant and creative she could be, with how powerful a presence. That's how I think about you, both of you, Arwad and you.

But that wasn't my question.

What was it, then?

Does a father see anything else in his daughter, or daughters?

When I hear that my daughters are beautiful and clever and so on, it makes me feel delighted and proud . . .

Right, it flatters you.

It makes me happy.

Of course!

And I think about the responsibility of people who have something to say and the urge to create. I wonder how my girls are going to approach that responsibility, how they will handle it and measure up to it, in order to make something profound out of it, as I did . . .

Yes, but that wasn't my question. I wanted to know whether the fact of being a father, or having become one, automatically slotted a filter in front of your eyes so that you become unable to see your daughter sitting here in a short skirt with her long legs and high heels. Don't you ever think, 'Good legs she's got' or something like that . . . I don't know . . .

No, I don't think anything of the sort.

Why not?

Because I've had my fill of trouble with women —

Expand a bit more, I don't get it. I want to know if fathers develop a biological filter. I want to understand how a father, on account of being a father, becomes blind to his daughter's body — her womanly body. Can desire ever enter into the equation? I want to know what goes on in a father's mind!

Isn't it hard for fathers not to behold in their daughter something other than 'a daughter'? Such as, a woman?

As a body, you mean?

That's right, yes, as a body!

But beauty is part of the body, is it not?

Exactly, so how do you deal with that?

I want you to take the greatest care of your body, I want you to be beautiful, and to not devalue that body . . . I wish that you wouldn't offer it to non-entities instead of to a man who deserves it. I worry about this often. When I find that my daughter has spent the night or been living with someone second-rate, who's unworthy of her, it makes me sad. In the same way I'm delighted if I see her going out with a pleasant, intelligent fellow. I'm unhappy when my 'brilliant' daughter appears to sell herself short; when she underestimates the value of her body and her personality.

Fear not, you don't have that problem with us two!

[LATER . . .]

So, do you think fathers have a filter over their eyes to avoid seeing their daughters when they're dressed to kill for a date with their boyfriend? If a father flies into a rage and packs a girl off to change because she looks like a whore, for instance, couldn't it be because he'd felt turned on by her at first? As if he'd said to himself, 'If she has that effect on me, what will she do to other men!' Of course, I'm overstating it a bit . . .

I would never react like that. I might tell you off if I didn't think your outfit was very nice! (*Smiles.*)

But don't you think that when a father acts that way, it could mean that he was fancying his daughter, especially if she's revealingly dressed?

There may be fathers like that, but I'm not one of them. If I see you turned out for a date, I'm only interested in how smart you look! (*Laughter.*)

Oh! Right! (Laughter.)

What's it like when you as a father see your little girl grow up and start dating a boy, and you can guess that they've gone all the way? How do you manage not to think about this body you 'created', this body you cuddled and nuzzled and watched grow, in the arms of another man? When a father catches a glimpse of her bare paunch, say (it's a woman's body, after all), doesn't he start picturing the way her boyfriend might fondle her, the way they kiss? Especially if he was the kind of dad to tickle his little girl's tummy . . . Does it come naturally, or is it an effort? Maybe it's in order to block out such imaginings that men in traditional societies forbid young girls to show too much flesh, to go out with boys before marriage, to lose their virginity and all that.

If the fellow in question is —

I know what you're going to say: if he's 'brilliant' enough . . .

. . . then I'll be delighted, but if he's an ass, well, I'll be most upset! (*Laughter.*)

There you are, it's because you're projecting yourself into him! He mustn't be an ass, because then he'd no longer correspond with your image!

Having said that, there's no logic in love. A woman can fall for a stupid person and so can a man. But speaking for myself, much as I believe that love lies outside reason and love is blind, I would still hope for my daughter to choose a man who deserves her.

Come on, doesn't it throw you just a little to see a boy's hands on your daughter's hips? Those hips that came from yours, that flesh you used to stroke when she was little?

Not at all, quite the reverse. I'll cheer when I can see my daughter with a man she loves.

Plenty of other fathers find it hard to compartmentalize the way you do.

They put pressure on their daughters . . .

Some even beat them and make their lives a misery . . .

Those are pathological cases.

Of course they are. But answer the question I put to you before: wouldn't you say that when highly traditional societies forbid young girls to show too much of their bodies or to go out with boys before marriage and risk their virginity, it's in order to avoid imagining certain things?

No, I would say it derives from tradition . . . a tradition which still continues, by the way. A girl who's known a lot of men will have trouble finding one for keeps, to marry. A fellow will go out with her, but he won't propose.

Yes, I know.

So perhaps that's why such 'measures' were taken: to save young girls from ruining their future prospects. In traditional societies, as you know very well, a woman can't live independently of men. Such societies cannot conceive of a woman enjoying financial independence, being responsible for her actions, living on her own, choosing the man she wants to love or with whom she simply wants to spend the night . . . Because of this, they treat young girls as though they were incapable of conducting their own lives. They regard females as eternal 'minors'. The only possible future for a girl is that of a spouse.

So it becomes impossible to marry off a girl who's

had any previous romantic or sexual entanglements. The main reason for this, I think, is that daughters are seen as chattels and not as free and independent beings. That's why their fathers behave so strictly and severely with them. Their one ambition is to pair the girl off with someone who comes from a prosperous, well-known family and, in order to do that, she has to be 'locked up' at home, as a way of signalling her virginity!

In other words a daughter is an investment, a capital that has to make a profit?

Yes, for her own good.

No! For the father's good!

For the sake of her future . . .

But that future is tied up with the rules of the society in which she lives! (Insistently.) Do you think a father could ever have a genuine love affair with his daughter? A wild, passionate affair?

No 'normal' person can engage in a passionate relationship with himself; it must be with a different body, different from his own. His daughter is 'himself'; she is his own body, in a sense. Such a relationship could never be anything but unwholesome. There could be no room for love in it. Love brings differences, opposites, together. It can't unite a person with himself . . .

It's a Man's Man's Man's World
(JAMES BROWN, 1966)

NINAR: *Before we go on, I'd like to point out that you've been very well-behaved so far, and the responses you've given fall somewhat on the 'conventional' side! It's funny—I set out to look for Adonis the man, and I keep bumping into the father! Anyhow, let's go on . . . Can man escape his destiny, do you think? Can he be authentically free, without setting boundaries for himself or leaning on crutches like religion, money or sex? Even though I myself consider sex to be 'divine', a form of nirvana . . . I reckon the war proved to the Lebanese that God was an illusion but, like the good Mediterraneans that they are, they couldn't accept that idea so they went on pretending He exists and believing in Him. In fact, their pious fervour was redirected—now the Lebanese should declare the Dollar to be their new God! They should raise green paper statues! The scramble for wealth is staggering!*

ADONIS: The Lebanese love of money is an ancient phenomenon, dating from long before the civil war. And
the Lebanese are not the only people devoted to making
money. Money offers them the sensation, the illusion
that they are free and don't need anybody else. When
they haven't got it, they feel as though they are in
chains. Economic deprivation is a form of slavery. Mind
you, total freedom doesn't exist, or not without certain
rules, and it's a relative concept that varies according to
culture, religion and custom. There is a small margin
of freedom within which one can always operate, provided one can afford it. Some are frightened by it, and
don't dare venture that far. As a general rule, however,
we have to ask ourselves how free anyone can be within an unfree society. It's a very complicated issue . . . All
we can say for sure is that there's no such thing as
absolute freedom. Talking of freedom, *Le Monde* was
banned from appearing in the UK yesterday!

Really? Why?

Because it contained an article about Prince Charles's
sex life.

That's unbelievable!

There's always a limit somewhere . . .

I wasn't talking about that kind of freedom.

You can never be completely free.

*In other words, you're always forced to subscribe to some
religion or ideology?*

You are where religion is allied to the state, making it a matter of public interest. Where that's the case you can't criticize religion, you can't say what you think of it out loud, spontaneously. It's forbidden to leave the Islamic faith, for example. If you forsake your religion, any Muslim has the right to kill you . . .

Yes, I know.

If someone is poor, how can he possibly be free? Freedom implies the fulfilment of desires. As for freedom in the sense of expression, that's a different problem again.

I meant to talk about human freedom. Can a person go through life without boundaries? Without religion?

Lots of people do. I'm one of them. I don't hold with religion.

Nor do I, so therefore it is possible to live without depending on a religion, or on money?

You can live without religion, but you can't live without money.

Money is more powerful than religion, in that sense. Basically, you're saying that we're inescapably slaves to something for as long as we live!

Not slaves, exactly. Freedom is always qualified by rules. There are lesser rules and greater rules—it all depends on the society, the culture, the individual. You can't begin to think about being free if you haven't got a job or any cash in your pocket, because that necessarily makes you dependent upon other people. The point is, you bring about your own freedom through your work. Freedom comes with responsibility. And if you can't express your thoughts in proper fashion, how do you expect to be free? We should be specific about the type of freedom we mean. Man is born free, but society has placed him in chains, as Rousseau would have it.

I see!

Yet how can we live outside society?

So it's society that lays down the rules?

The constraints come from within society . . .

Could religion be a constraint because it's a device for getting, and keeping, a grip on power?

Religion and money are inseparably linked. Religion has often been a means of seizing power, and it can't seize power without access to funds. As I see it, religion has been, and still is, one of the foremost instruments for getting into power and controlling society.

[SOME HOURS LATER . . .]

Do you think that a man (in the masculine sense) can ever love a woman who doesn't remind him of his mother, in one way or another?

No doubt about it. He can love a woman who doesn't remind him of his mother in the least.

And yet I've noticed this over and over again! A woman often looks physically very like her partner's mother. And the resemblance can go beyond the physical: the two may even behave in similar ways. As if what he'd really been looking for was a second Mummy.

Possibly, yes . . . or she might look like his daughter, or some other member of the family. However that may be, I reckon that anyone who marries a person who reminds them of their father or mother must have a personal or psychological problem.

Do you think two people can love each other, for a long time, without either of them recognizing a parental figure in the other?

There may be the odd case of what you say. But if you're asking the question of me, I am only capable of having a relationship with someone who is utterly different, both from myself and from my parents.

Can love outside marriage survive the passage of time, and exist in the absence of any project to have children?

Nothing lasts for ever. Neither love inside marriage, nor love outside marriage.

So I hear! I've been told this before, and oddly enough it's always been by men! (Smiles.)

Every aspect of love is contingent upon the condition and circumstances of the people involved. It's extremely rare for a love story to last until the end.

Well, of course I don't mean they have to be as madly in love throughout as on the first day. I'm just wondering if such a relationship can be sustained, so to speak.

It can—it turns into companionship. I doubt that a passionate romance between two people ever endures for very long. Everything must change and become transformed, since human beings themselves are always changing.

That's true, there's nothing stable. Seen from that point of view, it's quite reassuring!

[LATER . . .]

Take two people who once loved each other to distraction, shared absolutely everything, and then broke up . . . For some reason or other they become friends, and continue to see each other. Well, I can't do that. To break up with a man I adored, to whom I gave my all, with whom I shared everything—it's like being bodily torn away from him. Once I've torn myself away I can no longer give him anything, because it seems that my body, my heart and my brain work in unison. As long as I still love him, I want to be with him. I can't be doing with half-measures . . . And I don't think two people who love each other can ever split up. It's just not possible! If they do separate, it can only be because one of them is prepared to sacrifice the other—because it suits one of them. What are your thoughts on that?

I don't understand it either, but it's a thing that can happen . . . A love affair may evolve into an amicable, 'cool' relation, clear of hate or hostility; but it couldn't turn into a solid friendship.

If there's no more trust, how could we ever switch to being best friends? I don't get it! I've noticed that women are stronger and braver than men . . . I'm not referring to acts of heroism at times of danger or in war, I mean when it comes to difficult emotional situations. I find that women are more courageous, capable of dropping everything for the sake of a man and starting a new life elsewhere. This is a very feminine trait, it seems to me. I've also noticed that men who are comfortable with their feminine side often display the same strength of character. What's your relationship with your 'feminine side'? Do you find it scary?

Women have to be strong. Because a woman who is too 'easy' around men will suffer the consequences in her life. A woman has to be very strong and only surrender her body to a person she truly loves. And if this relationship fails, she should pause, take stock and think very carefully before giving her body to anyone else.

But that's not what I asked you, that wasn't the question at all!

That is why a woman has to be stronger than a man.

Do you mean that's what makes her stronger? Or that is what forces her to be stronger?

If she's an 'easy lay', her life is going to become very difficult indeed. She will forfeit the esteem of the men around her.

You mean that a woman has to be strong despite herself, in order to overcome all the problems thrown at her by a backward and traditional society?

It's true within modern societies as well . . . For, what do we mean by a modern society? A great city where nobody knows anybody else, where nobody knows who's been to bed with whom . . .

No, it's also a question of upbringing. The size of the city is neither here nor there.

In rural areas, people talk about this sort of thing when they have their gatherings. Everyone knows who's getting up to what and with whom, whether a woman is married or not . . .

It's a question of education, I tell you! In the East, in Arab countries at least, boys are brought up by their mother. And she, in spite of being a woman herself, drums it into her son that he must marry a virgin, a pure unsullied girl and whatnot. It's the mother who instils these ideas, not the father! It's insane!

Because she knows from experience that a woman who has been with more than one man in her life can never be faithful and honest towards the man she eventually marries . . .

That's a really silly thing to say! A woman who has known several men has got a bit of experience, she knows about pleasure and how to give it. Not like some poor girl who finds herself lying rigid in a bed without a clue!

Yes, but if she gets married after all that experience, she'll never be faithful . . .

That type of reasoning is extremely mistaken and danger-ous. A girl can easily not have known any men and be a vir-gin, and then, once she's married and a virgin no longer, start sleeping around! It happens all the time in Eastern societies, because of sexual frustration . . .

Those women enjoy their freedom in secret. Their freedom cannot be acknowledged by society at large.

For me, the mindset of a mother who instructs her son to marry a virgin borders on racism, it's misogynous at the very least! A woman's integrity doesn't reside in her sex!

All right, it's probably the wrong way to look at it.

Of course it's the wrong way! Fidelity has nothing to do with virginity!

It's because these societies equate maidenhood with purity. A man expects to be the first, the first man she meets and the first man to sleep with her. The fact that he's the first is thought to guarantee mutual trust, the happy development of the relationship, et cetera.

The happy development of a love affair or a marriage is not conditional on the girl's purity or virginity! It depends on the man's behaviour to her, and vice versa. A relationship will work out if the man is in love with his wife, if he knows how to care for her, if he is sensitive to her physically, if he makes love to her with his whole body and heart and shares with her all his longings and passions, the things that matter to him. The same goes for the woman . . . But if a man would rather save himself the bother, if he doesn't 'deliver', if he's incompetent or impotent or despises women, then that's another story. One can't reduce a woman's fidelity to her virginity, one can't reduce the extraordinary beauty of a relationship to 'the first time'! The wife's subjection for ever-more constitutes the dearest wish of all retrograde men. It's essential for a couple to have 'carnal knowledge' of one another before marriage, otherwise your unfortunate maiden may find herself hitched to a man who likes men and can't bear to touch her, condemning them both to a life of misery from which they can't escape!

Whereas the man can have had several premarital affairs, and no one says a word against that.

There's a huge inequality in that department.

No doubt about it.

But to go back to my earlier question. You haven't said anything about men who are at ease with their feminine side. Are such men stronger than those who haven't come to terms with their femininity?

One can't answer that kind of question out of hand, one can't make such sweeping theoretical judgements. Your questions are all too hypothetical, and so it's difficult for me to answer with precision. I can offer you my impressions, my personal opinion, but they won't have much to do with reality.

Another thing is that your questions tend to be pitched between two societies, one which is modern and one which is not. My hunch is that you're the one who has trouble with those two societies. It seems as if all your questions allude to the difficulties you're going through yourself.

Perhaps . . .

I don't have those kinds of problems.

You wouldn't, there's a difference of age, and anyway, you're a man.

I approach things differently, on another level . . .

It's obvious that there are two points of view here. If I had your age and your experience, I wouldn't be asking you these things. I'm only asking in an attempt to compare two worldviews, two experiences . . .

And that's why the answers can only be hypothetical.

Yes.

It's just my personal point of view . . .

But that's what I'm after, that's what I want!

It doesn't settle the issue . . .

Writing a sociological treatise about a society doesn't settle it either. There's nothing wrong with asking questions; solutions are another matter, aren't they?

I believe that every society operates on two levels: one that is exposed, and another that is secret and hidden. The hidden society enjoys the most freedom. But this secret plane is repressed and unacknowleged. It also comes in for much criticism from the visible, dominant plane, the stratum of laws, power and money. Here again, you can't make sweeping judgements, you can't compare one society with another; it's difficult. Each

society has its own way of operating, its peculiar style.
People often compare Damascus and Beirut, for example. Damascus harbours an incredible hidden society,
much richer than Beirut's — and yet Beirut is ostensibly
the freer city.

*It's probably because it's freer that Beirut doesn't have to
cultivate the hidden level. Whereas Damascus, being a very
conservative and traditional place, needs to have that alternative dimension. If you go to El-Hamidiya[1] in Damascus,
among all the craft knick-knacks like abayahs, hookahs,
incised copper trays, Korans and wooden boxes inlaid with
mother-of-pearl, you'll suddenly come across the most amazing saucy underwear . . . Stuff you wouldn't even find in
Pigalle! Ladies' panties with a slit through the crotch,
trimmed with fake fur and light-bulbs that start flashing at
the press of a button to the tune of 'Jingle Bells', 'O
Christmas Tree', 'Happy Birthday' or whatever . . .
Completely over-the-top! And you can't help wondering
what this kind of merchandise is doing in a working-class
market around the corner from the great mosque of the
Omeyyad dynasty! Who buys these things? Who wears
those panties? One is forced to conclude that some very
naughty things are going on in that city, despite the austere,
deeply unsexy and often extremely ugly look favoured by
bearded men and veiled women who never take off their
gloves or their long, drab overcoats, even when the temper-
ature's hitting forty-five degrees!*

*You asked me how I could compare two such different
environments, France and Lebanon — well, I can, easily,
because I am a product of both. The two cohabit inside me. I*

1 One of the largest
souks in the old quar-
ter of Damascus.

come from an Oriental, Arab society and I live in a Western society, in Paris.

All the same, they're pretty hard to compare. Because French society has been through its revolutions; it has accomplished the separation of Church and State, codified the law, and established a democracy. Lebanon, by contrast, is still a tribal, feudal society, a faith society. It hasn't had a revolution in the rational sense of the word, and there's no democracy . . . How can you compare the two? You can't!

Okay, but I'm not in a position to compare Lebanon to Saudi Arabia!

No, but you can't compare Lebanon to French society either!

That's the reason why every move towards greater freedom in that part of the world takes the form of a revolt against tradition, at the same time as it highlights the influence of Western models . . .

Yes, it's true. (Returning to the fray.) *Now then, tell me about your 'feminine side'!*

I don't go out of my way to emphasize it, and yet I can't suppress it. It's very apparent, it's manifest in my relationships with both men and women. Many women love me for my femininity, and other women detest me for the same trait . . .

Are they undermined by it, do they feel as though their womanliness is forced to compete with your feminine side?

Once at a dinner party I heard you say that marriage as an institution was stupid or uninteresting. I said to you, 'If that's so, then tell me, why are the most interesting men so often married?' (I don't wish to generalize, of course.) How do you explain that mystery?

They get married for reasons of conformity and self-interest. It's a social custom. You can't get away from it, and you can't fight it.

Meaning that one says one thing, and ends up by doing another?

Two people might be friends, and just to ruin this friendship they get married. Sometimes the friendship between them persists in spite of marriage. But personally I prefer my relationships out of wedlock, because the institution of marriage can be suffocating, not to say fatal, for those of us with something to say.

But how can you say that to your children as they grow up? I was educated in a household where it was made clear to me that marriage, while not perhaps compulsory, was a necessary thing . . . How could you tell us what you don't believe? Or is it that one only gets married for the sake of society?

I never told you any such thing.

Not right now, but when I was younger . . .

I never preached about marriage to either of you . . .

Yes, you did. There was always this subtext about the social imperative of marriage.

I always wanted you girls to find 'suitable' boyfriends, not necessarily husbands. After that it was always going to be your choice, depending on your experience.

Like I said, the obligation to marry for the sake of society.

There's a case to be made for that. The institution of marriage is a social investment. Two people get along socially, so they decide to form a mini-business or partnership. Some couples achieve it, although their success may conceal a multitude of sins. Or else it becomes a handicap, as when the spouses only remain in the 'business' out of self-interest. They no longer care for each other but they continue to share a home, trying to get around the problem by leading separate lives.

Yes, that's what most couples do.

They fear that to sever their relationship could prove more dangerous or damaging than to stick together, even if it's without passion or love. And especially if the arrangement contains positive advantages for the two people involved.

That's crazy, I think! Better to live with a friend from the start and take a lover, that's what I think!

[ANOTHER DAY . . .]

How does a person stop feeling homesick for the country, if they were born in a village and grew up in the midst of nature, among animals, with a particular relationship to the people around them? And then they go off to school in a town, moving further and further away from the village. How did you cope with that? In my case, having left Beirut, which is a small town compared to Paris (Beirut would fit into a single Parisian neighbourhood!) it took me ten years to get used to this gigantic new space, to the distances, to the architecture . . . I felt as though my body itself had to experiment and adjust its notions of scale by being here. Like when you're little, you think the school playground is enormous, and so is your house, and the terrace you always played on . . . And when you return to your childhood haunts as an adult, you discover to your amazement that the famous playground wasn't really so big after all . . .

I would have loved it if there'd been a school in my village. If there had been one, I'd have stayed. If there'd been an environment that could provide what I needed. But I was forced to go away from the village so as to bring forth my own energy, find myself a position, and grow. But having accomplished all that, I find that nowadays I do everything I can to go back there and spend some time. I talk to the people I once lived with, the people I grew up with, I visit the fields where I used to work . . . Sadly, my childhood home is no longer standing. But I love being back in the midst of all that . . .

What was your state of mind, the very first time you left the village and headed off to town?

I stopped thinking about the village, I didn't like going back there. But now that I've made something of my life, now that I have a presence in the world . . .

Now that you're strong . . .

I keep remembering the old place, and trying to reconnect with the childhood I had over there, with childhood memories . . . My childhood was extremely rich in some respects.

Has that environment not changed? Didn't you have trouble recognizing the same place?

Oh yes, everything's changed. The surroundings I remember seemed vast at the time.

Because you were so small? What does the village represent for you? You spent your first fifteen years there, didn't you? What do you expect from it now, after nearly sixty years away?

Memory. It's a storehouse of memories, and to me memory is an essential component of life, of the spirit, of the emotions. I feel that I was born within that memory and that I'm going to have to die there. To die in the place where I was born. Therefore the country isn't merely the place where I came into the world — it's also the place where I shall take my leave of it.

Why?

I can't explain it, but that's my intuition. When I die, I should like to be buried there. It's the cradle from which I first contemplated life, and I'd like to return to it. Other people would say the reverse, and so I do realize how personal this is. I can well understand the desire to be cremated and have one's ashes scattered somewhere, over the waves or to the winds . . . But I want to be buried in my corner of the countryside.

But why?

I don't know, that's just the way it is.

I'm trying to understand. Can a native place, a birthplace, exert so much more of a pull than a place where one wasn't perhaps born, but where one loved, and worked and lived?

That's why I said it was personal. I think it's a question of roots. A return to one's roots . . . a way of looping the loop, as it were, coming back to the point of departure.

But life and death are intertwined in any case, or they will be, ultimately, whether it's in the same place or not.

Yes, but that would be like having one thing placed in a dish, and another thing placed outside the dish. The difference is a purely formal one, no doubt, but it's essential nonetheless.

It would make you feel more secure, do you mean?

But we don't feel anything at all after death!

Exactly, all the more reason!

It has to do with the subconscious, I can't really analyse it. That's why I say it's a question of personal conviction. I have no problem with anyone wishing to be buried far from the place of their birth.

Like me, for instance. I was born in a hospital, so it would make no sense for me . . . What I want is to be cremated and for my ashes to be scattered over the Mediterranean sea. It has huge symbolic significance for me.

You always say that 'identity' is something we create for ourselves, that it's in perpetual flux, and therefore independent of our national origins. So why should the village, or the birthplace, be so important? These notions of 'soil' and 'nationality' reduce people to slavery, rendering them dependent on the powers that be . . .

Slavery? Nonsense, it's a very natural instinct.

Your identity evolved and changed, you enriched it . . .

That was my choice, nothing to do with identity and its evolution. Look at Edward Said, for instance: he wasn't buried in Jerusalem but in the Lebanese mountains, in the same cemetery as his wife's family. You can never choose the place of your birth, but that of your death, you can. That's what I'm doing: I'm choosing the place of my death.

Yes . . . I don't know. I don't understand it.

It's not to be understood, it's not a logical proposition.

I bow to your decision, but I can't understand it. Unless it's a matter of recognition. In fact, you've been recognized and acclaimed by the whole world in one form or another. All that's left is this patch of earth, your village, which will be the last place to recognize you – the final witness.

[LATER . . .]

By leaving your village at the age of fourteen, you were, in a sense, prompting your 'destiny'. In the same way, by standing up to recite your poem (on 22 March 1944) to the then President of the Republic on his tour of the Syrian coastal region, and asking for his help to go to school, you were conquering your independence, among other things, and detaching yourself from the traditional Arab family network. You found yourself alone, and more so when you lost your father quite soon after. It must have been very tough for you. Wasn't there a slightly bitter taste to your freedom?

No, on the contrary, it taught me a great deal.

Did it enrich you, did it liberate you?

It gave me a greater freedom, and it taught me to rely on myself. I learnt to construct myself, to be independent and to embrace hard work. My departure changed my life. For I'm sure that had I stayed I would have turned into a peasant, like the others! It was chance that made me.

You never say much about your father's reaction to your success with the President. What did he think about your going to school?

He was very glad about it, he was delighted.

And what did he say?

That he was proud of my initiative, that it had brought him great joy.

That must have made you feel good, even if you lost him afterwards, too soon for him to see you succeed and become a poet. Perhaps the excitement you both shared that day (the fact that he was there to witness your victorious breakthrough) goes some way towards consoling you for his not being around to see you now.

No, actually, it's something that grieves me even more. I wish we could have seen more of each other, I wish we'd known each other better. For my part, I didn't know him at all! And that's why he's always in my mind, forever by my side, as though I were trying to compensate for this loss that came too soon . . .

2 Elia Suleiman (b. 1960): Palestinian filmmaker, born in Nazareth.

Once I heard Elia Suleiman[2] answering journalists' questions after the screening of his film Divine Intervention *(which won the Grand Jury Prize at Cannes in 2002). He said something that was very beautiful and right: 'I became a "Jew", but in contrast many Jews in Israel have lost their "becoming-Jewish".' I'm fascinated by this idea of 'becoming'. That's why I'm reading* A Thousand Plateaus *by Deleuze and Guattari. I can't make head or tail of it so far! But I'm not giving up, because I'm very intrigued by this business of 'becoming-woman' and even more, needless to say, by the business of 'becoming-animal'! What about you, what 'becoming' are you in? In what direction were you pushed by exile, or the attacks on you?*

Wherever I have been, I've passed through that place on my own. I wouldn't put down roots, I made no attempt to insert myself. I have lived at arm's length from every place and, while this may have caused me certain problems, it also empowered me. I didn't merge with my surroundings but I didn't challenge them either, and perhaps that's why people have been led to refer to my 'non-love' of stability . . . It's not oneself who creates one's country (nation, homeland, whatever you want to call it). Only animals have a genuine rapport with the territory in which they live. In that sense, I feel more of a kinship with migrating birds. I lack all sense of attachment to a place, to a land. This 'place', this land, they travel with me.

All the same, you've decided to die – to be buried – in the place of your birth. Isn't that a contradiction?

No, because death means the end of movement: I'll have no choice but to keep still!

Yes . . .

Wherever I went, I invented my own location.

I tend to get attached to places that allow me to flourish, to work, to engage in all my various activities. If I'm somewhere that withholds those things from me, I pack my bags and strike out in search of a more auspicious setting . . .

For me, a place is a space that moves with me. I've said this many a time, my 'motherland' is my language . . . the language in which I write.

Je T'aime Moi Non Plus

(SERGE GAINSBOURG AND JANE BIRKIN, 1969)

NINAR: *How has poetry helped you to live, to survive? Or perhaps it wasn't as important as all that?*

ADONIS: I believe that poetry and writing have offered me a kind of compensation for the lack of 'motherland' and native soil. My connection to the world of language is stronger than the one I have to people and places. This may well be a failing on my part, or a mistake, but it's the way it is. I never make a connection with a place as such, but only with the thread that binds me to it. This thread is the link that leads me to discover myself, that allows me to apprehend myself more fully. And I can only attain that by means of language . . .

This language, then, is being created by you and is creating you, both at the same time?

Precisely.

117

What is the part played by language at this moment in your life? Has its role changed over the years? Do you feel a greater need for it now than before? Do you feel you've come to master it, or that it eludes you more and more?

It depends on the relationship one has with oneself. Since my identity is constantly changing, I have a two-fold sensation about this. On the one hand this identity must occupy a space and on the other, it's crying out for time to find its place. Therefore time becomes more important than place. And therefore I am in a tragic relationship with time, because I feel I need so much of it and yet there is so little of it left . . . As a result, I feel that I've lost a huge part of myself on the days I don't manage to work. As you get older, you feel you're running out of time to say what you needed to say. It's a terrible feeling, especially when you have a lot to say and you are perfectly in control of your material. Sometimes it seems as though the more I progress, the less I achieve, and I haven't done all that I had to do. All this fills me with a sense of tragedy.

What has writing poetry really done for you?

I've already answered that question, by saying that poetry has given me a knowledge of myself and a better knowledge of the world around me. Above all, it's helped me to live my life better.

Did you choose the domain of poetry, or were you influenced by your father's passion for ancient Arabic verse – like something forced on you at first but which you grew to love?

I was born into favourable surroundings for the encounter with poetry. My father was himself a poet, and it was he who first taught me the art. I was born into poetry, I was moulded by poetry. But I soon turned away from this primary form. The form evolved and changed into something unprecedented and unrecognizable . . .

You mean that at first it was taken for granted?

I no longer have anything in common with what I was in the past. My poetry has completely changed.

In other words you took it for granted at first, it was the obvious thing.

Yes, like my birth . . .

How does someone know if their writing is any good? How can you tell whether what you've written is good, singular or new? Is it something that you feel inside, or do other people help you to see it?

Let's deal with the external element first. Another person's reactions and way of reading can afford you a measure of the importance and value of what you're doing. Having said that, I also believe that poets and creators are their own best sounding-boards, the best judges of their own worth. Because they belong to the same context. When you write a poem, you're comparing it, consciously or otherwise, to what other poets have done with the same language. In the light of this comparison, you'll know whether what you've written is different, you'll know whether you've achieved something fresh or not . . . So I think that the only possible judge is the poet himself. If he's honest, he will be the first critic of his own work.

I think that's true for every creator.

Nobody can understand a work better than its author.

How necessary is it to receive encouragement from other people? Do you discuss your poems or your new ideas with your friends? Or with anyone? Is it important to run new ideas past other people, or is it preferable to consult them once the thought is mature and down on paper?

Long ago, I was in the habit of reading my poems to friends before I published them. Not any more. I say what I have to say, without going back over it.

To what extent do artists of any kind need a critical response from the general public, or from specialists?

As far as I'm concerned, the public means nothing. The notion of the public is a myth. Not only that, it's a word with fundamentally commercial connotations, these days. The public consists of a large number of individuals, each of them distinct from the rest. Thus if you go down well with the public, it implies that you've foregrounded the 'common' dimension of your work rather than its 'uniqueness'. That's why I've no time for the 'public'. I'm only interested in the person, the individual, the reader. In any case one doesn't write

to be read, one doesn't even write to express oneself—
I don't hold with that idea. Because you can't express
all the things you are. You write, you create, the better
to know yourself, the better to understand yourself . . .
to understand the world a little more.

To act and react with regard to the world, to society?

Now, if people react to my work and appreciate it,
that's fine. If they don't appreciate it, that's fine by me
as well. There are plenty of artists and writers who
produce for the public. I don't.

[A FEW HOURS LATER . . .]

Now for a somewhat clichéd question: do you think it's pos-
sible to be both a mother and an artist? Can a woman be a
great writer or a great painter once she has started a family
and had children? My view is that it comes down to a prob-
lem of time management, and to the sense of urgency. If I
feel that I exist principally in and through my children, I
won't have the same drive, the same need to create. This may
be a deceptive problem, just another excuse to put women
down or to guilt-trip them by saying that a woman is a
mother first and foremost, and if she's not a mother then she
must be 'sterile'.

Well, look at Bach, he had a large family . . .

I was talking about female artists.

Yes, of course it's possible.

But there aren't many outstanding women artists who had children, are there?

On the contrary, a woman's highest genius can be brought to fruition by her maternal feelings.

(Doubtfully) . . . ?

Or maybe not. Again, it depends on the woman.

More often it's not.

There are no hard and fast rules.

If you say so . . . I don't know, I have my doubts.

The same goes for men.

Why are there more male artists than female artists, then?

As an absolute quantity, there are more male artists. Because women, historically and socially speaking, have rarely had the chance to dedicate themselves singlemindedly to their art. And because art demands relentless commitment, and a woman can only give herself up completely to her child, which is her most successful creation.

Ha, you see! Even you, you just said it: 'her most successful creation'!

I'm talking about the child, because she chose to have it.

Oh, right!

There are people whose one and only dream in life is to produce a little creature from their bellies, something for them to gaze at and to bring up. To me this indicates a stunted creative impulse.

Yes.

Then there are women who bear children out of habit, even when their main interest in life centres on their art or their creative goals.

But if you do have children, how can you pay more attention to your work than to them?

Well, I always managed to do that.

I know, but you're a father, and I'm talking about mothers. Mothers have a different relationship with their children.

That's true, and it's a problem, but there are women who both write and have children. Mind you, we'd have to take a good look at the quality of their writing, or of their visual art.

Of course, because anyone can write or paint or make movies, but I'm thinking of those women who are truly obsessed with it.

An admirable obsession . . .

Yes, because it's all about where you choose to put your energies!

Great women in history —

Didn't have children . . .

Didn't have successful conjugal lives.

Virginia Woolf, for instance, did she have children?

I don't know.

She was obsessed by her work all her life, wasn't she? You look at a woman like that and you wonder how she could have done it if she'd been a mother! Her kids would have pined away! You can't pour your energies into domestic life (husband, children and all that) and have any left over for your work . . . It's appalling but it's a fact.

Yes, it's a real problem.

So women are faced with a hopeless choice. Either to have children and be unable to devote themselves entirely to their art, or to be an artist and sacrifice the possibility of motherhood.

It's not so cut and dried . . .

Do you realize how strong, how tireless a woman has to be? She has to put in three times the effort of anyone else.

She needs to have a forceful personality.

And extensible time, somehow! You've got to divide your time into separate compartments.

Yes, it requires an exceptional woman for sure.

[SOME HOURS LATER . . .]

What are the limits of poetry? Where are its borders? Can it

withstand upheavals, transformations, stylistic revolutions?
Or must it comply with certain rules?

One peculiarity of art, whether it's poetry, sculpture or painting, is that there are no rules, no limits whatsoever. The artist sets his own rules, and there are times when he can overturn all the assumptions of art or poetry. No one can rightly declare that what he produces is art or not art. This exemption from boundaries and definitions is surely one of the greatest mysteries of the creative process. Art exists in perpetual motion, always renewing itself, and its rules are a function of this. Therefore I see no limits to poetry. Even non-poetry can be poetry.

How would you describe your relationship to the Arabic language? Is it your work-tool, your identity, your body, your soul?

I can't imagine myself in any other language. Arabic lives in me, so much so that it has become jealous of all other tongues. And I believe that this deep-rootedness of Arabic in me has made me a dunce for other languages. I've loved it so much that it loves me back — it wraps itself around me and prevents me from learning any other tongue . . .

I've felt that about you . . .

A friend once said, after she heard me speak my poetry: 'You don't need a woman, you're making love to the language!' She was right!

What kind of relationship would you advise me to entertain with it? Because this is something that worries me a lot. I can write a little Arabic, but not enough. The language hangs over me like a duty or a burden. It's like a lover I've neglected and who keeps stalking me. At the same time I feel that I should learn to master it, in order to get closer to you and to preserve my Arab identity. I feel torn between these two attitudes. I keep thinking that it would tell me so much about you! Isn't that weird!

Yes, I see your problem, but I can't sort it out for you. You must tackle it by yourself, because it's impossible to understand a poet without having a perfect grasp of the language he writes in. Translation can go some of the way towards providing access—it'll convey the thoughts, the images, the overall idea, and even the sense of a particular poetics—but if you truly want to understand a poet, you have to read him in his mother tongue. Translation has its limits, and in a sense that's the wall you're up against.

But how well would I have to know Arabic?

You would have to know it to perfection. And it's unlikely that by now you could ever reach that level.

What's the upper limit? Who can define that level?

No language can ever be possessed in its totality. It can only be partially possessed. A language is like a receding horizon, towards which we advance ad infinitum. The more we advance, the more our knowledge of the language seems to shrink . . . But there is also a social issue involved, for we were born in the lap of the language that constitutes our skin, our veins, our blood. If we haven't suckled it from the very first instant, we shall never learn it. Oh, we'll be able to speak it, to read it, but we shall not really be able to write in it. Because this language is like the first wail of a new-born, it's the first sobbing cry. You as a creator, as an artist yourself, should be able to command one language to that standard. Now, you can opt for French if you like, but then there will always be a barrier between us, a poetic and linguistic barrier, and you'll have to accept it and it mustn't distress you too much. I don't know which your language is for howling and weeping in, whether it's Arabic or French; however, I rather think Arabic will always remain your language of culture, as opposed to a mother tongue . . .

And especially as I sometimes feel that you make up such an indestructible couple, you and Arabic! Welded together, for better or for worse . . . Or sometimes it's as if the language were your sister, and your father had entrusted her to you, asking you to take precious care of her, to love her and live with her and do everything in your power to make her beautiful and fulfilled . . . She glows in your hands, and especially on your lips. She is like a wife, a sister and a daughter to you all in one. Needless to say she's the only woman I'm truly jealous of, because she's so utterly gorgeous, potent and tender, she's sparkly, wilful, impassioned, violent, refined; she is poetry, she is sophistication, marvellous and bewitching, in your mouth, against your palate, on your

tongue and deep inside your throat . . . The words imbibe
your saliva, becoming moist and warm . . . As they leave
your mouth they rush into it once more, it's a never-ending
movement, you recreate them again and again. The same
word, spoken by you and by another, is not the same . . .
With other people there's a deficit of meaning, whereas with
you there's always a surplus. You do what you like with
words, you can sculpt them or send them spinning as you
please. When I listen to you recite your poems, what a tango
I hear, mixed up with flamenco and a dash of Eastern dance
. . . Strains of passion, desire, sensuality and sorcery . . .

It's true. And this can erect a screen between me and
my Arab readers, because they can't capture this
speaking tongue of mine, so as to understand it
through and through.

I think that for someone to truly grasp your poetry, they
have to realize that it's an act of lovemaking, that there's lit-
erally a carnal relationship between you and your language.
It's not so much the words themselves that need to be under-
stood, it's your bond with the Arab language. People have
got to bear in mind that these are not just words, these are
words uttered by you . . .

What you're saying there is very important. Did you
think of it yourself?

Yes, because it's obvious, I can hear it, I can see it . . .

1 That which is pro-
hibited, sinful.

And can you see how the Arab tongue has enclosed
me in a *haram*?[1]

She's your lover.

She draws a *haram* around me, she manoeuvres so as to keep me beyond the reach of my readers and prevent them from comprehending me fully. When you look at most poets who write in this language, you begin to see that they are standing in one place whilst the Arab tongue is in another place . . .

And that's exactly why I now think that Arabic is you. It can't be any other way; even without reading your poems, I feel such a potent bond between the pair of you . . . I've never heard it spoken like that by anyone else alive. Of course, you can point me back to Al-Mutanabi[2] or I don't know who, but only poets who are dead.

2 Al-Mutanabi (915–965): considered to be the greatest of Arab poets.

Many people would agree with you. You're not the only one to have noticed. Everyone who hears me speak my poems confirms that this is something else, a different order of experience. They go on to say that no one but Adonis knows how to read a poem in all the Arab world.

In all the whole world, surely . . .

Today I read something very fine by Philippe Sollers.

About Beckett?

Yes, Beckett. His closing sentence runs: 'The voice is infused with the fragrance of truth.' Beautiful! Language as a voice. I very much liked that phrase!

When you take the language and read it aloud as I do, you can actually smell the fragrance of truth.

Once I heard you say that to verify the etymology of Arabic words, it was necessary to return to the dialect form. What did you mean by that? You were talking to Samir Amin, the economist.[3]

3 Samir Amin (b. 1931): Egyptian economist residing in Paris.

No, what I said was that most Arabic dialect words have roots in the literary language. And for that reason it's sometimes a good thing to defer to the vernacular, to let common parlance take precedence over the scholarly, literary register. Because words, like living beings, die and become obsolete. Plenty of poets are given to digging about in the graveyards of language in order to exhume dead words, but these come out as leaden and futile and, more importantly, they've become detached from general usage. That's why one should be careful only to employ words that still have living roots in everyday life. The problem of poetry is that words don't have a life of their own — they are caught in the yarns of a fabric. Poetry is also like a loom upon which words are to be woven together. The fabric materializes spontaneously, as though it were dictated by the words themselves.

Rock the Casbah
(THE CLASH, 1982)

NINAR: *Why, in your opinion, is there such an attachment in Arab countries to all that's traditional? I don't think all traditions are fit to be preserved, and I regard the people who cling desperately to the old ways as incapable of working for the future. In Europe, tradition was pushed to the background by revolutions. Have there been any revolutions driven by concepts of democracy, in Arab history? What about anarchism? Were they ever tempted? I know some uprisings took place, but they were against an occupier, an army or a colonizing power. Does the concept of revolution play any part in the mental or historical structures of Arab peoples?*

1 Abu Nawas (757–814): one of the greatest Arab poets and a famous libertine. He sang praises of wine and life's sensual pleasures.

ADONIS: Arab history is packed with revolutions, they've never stopped. Some were minor uprisings, of course, or revolts intent on imposing a different interpretation of Islam. But all of the Arab geniuses under Islam, from Abu Nawas[1] to al-Ma'ari, including the greatest poets and philosophers—all were opposed to

133

religion. No body of thought arose directly from religion, like perfume wafting from a flower. Scholars and poets used to elaborate new flowers, with a view to distilling a different fragrance. For that reason, strictly speaking, Islam as a religion lacks a religious literature. In the same way there's no such thing as an Islamic philosophy: there's a theology, and there's a Law, the sharia. The first explained the Koran and the second established laws and rules. But, aside from those texts, all of literature and all of poetry arose in opposition to religion. Every poet took himself for a prophet, proclaimed that his poetry was the best and that he was the scourge of religion. But all such writings were sidelined, unsurprisingly, because they offended against religion, religious morality and tradition.

But then why today . . .

Today, the revolutions are different. The dominant sector is always trying to prove that revolutions are under way in the name of Islam but, instead of this, to my mind, we find political skirmishes that lack the stature of total revolutions—ideological, philosophical and artistic revolutions. The kind that interest us and of which we speak here. Today's 'revolutions' confine themselves to making political demands on incumbent powers or external hegemonies, and therefore they are not revolutions.

Why are there no revolutions in the true sense of the word?

But there have always been people and groups who campaigned for secularism, who wanted progress.

When was this?

Throughout our present, contemporary history. All the parties as well as the intelligentsia called for these kinds of changes in every Arab country, but they lost the battle. They simply failed. Their ideas failed. Because the social tissue as a whole rejected those ideas.

But why?

The influence of religion was ultimately the stronger.

Tradition again . . .

Tradition, and religious institutions.

Why does European society—

For one crucial reason, which is: in Islam, religion is more than a simple question of belief; it's just as much a way of life. Religion is the cornerstone of marriage, culture, family life and everything else.

No different from Christianity or Judaism. With all monotheistic religions, you always get the same refrain: 'Thou shalt not do this, thou shalt do the other', 'Thou shalt not lie with thy wife like this, thou shalt lie with her like that!'

Yes, but once the revolution had been accomplished, the panorama changed. Europe more than anywhere has worked through its revolutions, but we can't say the same of the Arab world. A revolution is not something that can be invented overnight, it requires a conducive medium . . .

So what you're saying is that the sociocultural medium that prevails in the Arab-Muslim world is not conducive to this kind of revolution?

That's precisely it. Society isn't going to change or move forward in obedience to a handful of enlightened, progressive, secular revolutionaries! In Lebanon, for example, there are revolutionaries galore, and yet society hasn't changed in the slightest because of them. Society is never going to change so long as the institutions remain the same, the family structure remains the same, ditto the power structure. When institutions evolve, society follows suit. But it's impossible to change an institution by dint of ideas alone! A genuine revolution is what's called for, in which people accept change, institutional change in particular.

How are people ever going to accept change?

Given time, they might. But time is what it will take. You can't rustle up a revolution out of thin air.

The acceptance won't happen overnight. People need to be prepared.

That calls for a lengthy and persevering process, and it must be admitted that we've made little headway so far.

How might the process be fuelled?

By ideas. One can never repeat this too often. One must insist on discussing ideas, and not slacken off as soon as some small improvement occurs. There's a risk that for one reason or another, that small improvement may shortly be neutralized or undone.

And how do you explain all those lefty intellectuals, some of them from the far left in fact, who were reborn as 'Islamists' after the war? The mind boggles!

Well, their ideas were only skin-deep in the first place, not solidly anchored. They were politicians. The only thing they cared about was getting their hands on power. They fancied that once they were in power, they would be able to change everything. This proved to be an illusion. Because getting into power per se means nothing, and to do so, even when it's on behalf of the revolution, can engender more corruption than there was under the regime that was overthrown. The old parties, the so-called national parties that took over after independence, were paradoxically more progressive than the so-called revolutionary parties of today.

What's going on in the mind of someone who once belonged to the far left, and then becomes an Islamist?

Several factors are involved . . . In the first place, the ideological structure that characterizes the left in the Arab world. This mindset purports to know all the answers to all the questions—exactly like religion! In the Arab world, political parties develop into new religions. And you can't fight one religion with another. In order to combat religion you have to deploy ideas, values and a philosophy that's capable of dismantling the grounds for religion. But the left parties failed to undertake a historical analysis of the reasons that endow religion with the power and authority that it has. On the contrary, they are beguiled by power. They rose to power, and forgot about the masses. And that's why they failed.

You mentioned before that one of the preconditions for launching a revolution is institutional change. But isn't it also the case that Arab societies are becoming ever more inward-looking and hostile to hybridization? Isn't this mounting fanaticism just the last gasp of conservatism, before the inevitable moment of opening up? These societies are clearly moribund, as they're unable to renew themselves, and so the fanaticism might simply be their last, desperate stand.

Absolutely. There's a most deplorable regression. The racism is appalling too. Black people are still referred to as 'slaves'. And religious hegemony is advancing like a galloping tide. Religion is becoming more and more powerful, not just on the ideological plane but in terms of emotions and customs and private life. Some political parties say that all this will change as soon as we get into government! But they've been saying it for fifty years, it's been tried, and nothing ever changed. Since we have failed on all fronts, it's time to get back to the drawing board and think up some different solutions. All the same, the spark of rebellion, the spark of our demands, will never be completely stamped out. There are always two currents flowing through society: one conservative and one that aspires to change. There will always be a clash between these two visions. To bring about radical change, to launch a revolution, we need historic opportunities. We'll have to wait.

So you don't see any risk of implosion in these closed societies, in their refusal to change or to mingle?

Indeed I do, and it's one of the great problems of contemporary Arab societies. The concept of the 'Orient' itself is fading away. What's left of the Arab East? There is no more history of orientalism, for Arab society now forms part of the West. It no longer produces anything; it lives off the West, consuming the production of others.

Yes, it's true, the Arab East has become like a deprived shanty of the West. But the Arab East is still reluctant to admit it. They still go on about Arab identity, al-umma[2] and all that.

2 The Arab nation.

This illusion is shored up by religion. Arab societies avail themselves of every Western invention, claiming permission from God Himself! In all other respects we'll remain just as we are, thank you. It's an impossible contortion, and it can't last. But once again, it'll take a very long time, because a society that has existed like this for a millennium and a half is unlikely to change in the space of a year or two. You might be looking at another five hundred years!

In other words Arab societies are structured by Islam, their deep framework is provided by religion. Are there any other elements that contributed to structure them?

At bottom, Islam is a politico-religious structure.

What became of the culture that preceded Islam? Islam has only been around for about one thousand five hundred years . . . Before that, there was a different civilization. What did we inherit from that civilization – anything?

It was completely destroyed . . .

Completely? Didn't it leave anything behind?

Not a thing!

[LATER . . .]

I've noticed that many Arab women 'go to war' on their body hair. There's a venerable tradition of waxing it off. Women remove, or have someone remove for them, the hair not only from shins, thighs, armpits, and what they call the 'bikini line', but also from arms and forearms, and the whole pubis. It makes me wonder whether it's prescribed by the Koran . . . Anyway, someone told me that the Shia (both male and female) are expected to shave their bodies all over! Where do you think this hair obsession comes from? Is it to establish the maximum possible distance from animals? Or from uncleanliness? Why should body hair be considered unclean?

No, there could be another reason—it could be to make women look completely different from men.

Oh yes, it could be!

Men are the hairy ones. Women might think that this contrast is what attracts them. I would say it's a form of eroticism *avant la lettre*. A natural eroticism . . . Men don't like women to be hairy, they would look too similar.

That's really interesting, I'd never thought of it that way!

I'm sure that's the reason . . .

Yes, but it's such a hang-up. I know people who shave their arms, their whole bodies . . . Is it true that the Shia shave all over?

No, they grow long beards.

I'm not talking about beards.

They have no hard and fast rule against body hair.

And is that why some people are convinced that head hair is too indecent to be shown? Why some women take it on themselves to cover their heads with a scarf? Or is it simply because hair is liable to arouse thoughts of sex?

No, there are several explanations for the fact that women have to cover their heads. It might mean that they shouldn't socialize with men, for fear that something may happen. The saying goes that a man and a woman can never meet alone, for the devil will always turn up to make a threesome! There could be an attraction, it's thought. And they want to prevent that attraction from happening. However, there's no serious objection to a woman entertaining her own thoughts or fantasies . . . Sin and betrayal, in their minds, take place when bodies meet and merge. Sometimes a man—or a woman—can betray themselves in thoughts, in dreams, in feelings . . . but that's not a concern for them.

Don't you think that a woman with her hair covered, a veiled woman, is tantamount to a 'sex on legs'? Surely the very fact of wearing a veil underscores the idea that the head is a sex, a covered sex! Far from concealing this organ, they draw attention to it, they make it extra conspicuous. There was a great moment during a programme on France 2 called 'Campus', hosted by Guillaume Durand. Durand had invited the Lévy sisters on, both of whom wear headscarves, and were at the centre of the controversy about the headscarf in schools. One of the sisters declared: 'The headscarf is a sign of modesty. They can't tell us to take it off! How would you feel if someone ordered you to take off your underpants?'

I remember saying to someone once, 'Can't you see that the veil is designed to be worn exactly in the way that's most attractive to men? All it does is to show off the hair, the eyes, the mouth, to their best advantage!' But I do believe that in most cases it's a signal, to say: 'I am not like a Western woman.'

No, on the contrary, it's reducing a woman to one thing: her sex. As in, the specific sexual organ belonging to the wearer of the veil.

Yes, you're right.

Résiste

(FRANCE GALL, 1981)

NINAR: *Don't you think that the Islamic veil, the way it's worn at the moment, could equally be an inheritance from the Romans? The erotic frescoes in Pompeii, in the Villa of the Mysteries, included one object that everyone found mesmerizing — a huge phallus (the fascinus), and it was forever covered by a dark sheet to hide it from view. Pascal Quignard analyses this phenomenon of fascination very well in his book,* Sex and Awe:[1] *'Mystery occurs when awe is compounded by fascination. If there is to be fascination, the presence of a fascinus is necessary. The fascinus stands in the centre, covered by a dark cloth, in its sacred basket of woven rushes. The feeling of fearful, reverent awe couples the sense of being overwhelmed to that of being overcome.' Veiled women can surely be seen as a tremendous symbol of 'what must remain hidden, as it is an object of fascination and desire'. With a touch of the divine, as well, the divinity that cannot be looked upon directly. If I had to find some positive aspect to all this, I'd say that women become trans-*

1 Pascal Quignard, *Le sexe et l'effroi* (Paris: Gallimard, 1994).

formed into deities, a source of fascination for men and by the same token a source of fantasies.

ADONIS: That's very true. I remember once warning some friends in Europe: 'Don't be surprised at the sight of veiled women,' I told them, 'don't wonder at men wanting women to cover their heads, because the one and only rival to the image of God is Woman! And that's why men cover her up . . .'

Fine, I understand and I don't object, but then why do monotheistic religions show such violence against women? Is it merely a reflection of society? Or is there some other factor at work?

It's a 'tradition', based on a misleading, political interpretation of the Koran.

But why? And in every one of those religions! Among orthodox Jews, for instance, the man says 'Dear God, I thank you for not having made me a woman' as part of his morning prayer! I saw that in a film by Amos Gitai[2] called Kadosh, *which describes the private and social life of a Hassidic student, showing how he treats his wife and what it's like for her. It's quite harrowing to watch, very tough on the woman. And of course in Muslim families too you see some terribly harsh and cruel treatments.*

In Muslim societies, this repression is only on the level of religious legislation. Because, at the same time, Islam itself has always tolerated the right to pleasure—a man is welcome to marry four women, five

2 Amos Gitai (b. 1950): Israeli film director, born in Haifa.

women, ten women . . . With its care for sensuality and the joys of the flesh, Islam elevated women into objects of delight and desire, which a Muslim is entitled to physically possess for his enjoyment.

But the enjoyment is his, it's all for his benefit!

That's a good point, it does concern the man.

So there you are, there's the violence, the fact that every-thing is arranged around his pleasure, with no thought for hers!

But before Islam, women were free to marry and divorce as they liked, and no one ever prevented them or criticized them for it.

Before Islam, sure — but I was talking about monotheistic religions. Why do they oppress women like that?

Because they are patriarchal societies! The father is a stand-in for God and a woman can only follow behind, especially as she has no economic independence. She is one of the many things that revolve around the man. There are some glaring contradictions here. It is said, for example, that women are 'impure' (especially with regard to their bodies). Well, if women were really as soiled and polluted as all that, how could they be givers of life, bringing forth men like Jesus, or Prophet Mohammed? How could a woman ever give birth to a man of virtue? She is impure, she is evil, and yet she bears prophets and great men. Such contradictions don't make sense. In fact they're ludicrous.

147

But Prophet Mohammed was basically an ordinary man,
until he was chosen to be the mouthpiece of revelation. So
presumably his mother could have been anyone: it was God
who chose him . . .

Yes, that's what they say . . . one would have to be a
believer. I think that monotheistic religions were a
form of insurrection, like revolutions conducted
against the societies of the time. The monotheists were
clever about it because, rather than field destructive
armies, they found this other means to change society
and to control it. It's worth pointing out that all the
monotheistic religions disapproved of the spirit of
innovation and creation. Not one of them ever
matched the achievements of Sumer or Babylon or
Ancient Greece or the Pharaohs, in terms of art or
indeed in the domain of philosophy and poetry . . .
This shows that they were political enterprises, with
hegemonic goals, rather than profound existential
experiences.

How do you explain the fact that it's down to the woman to
guarantee the family honour? First through her virginity,
then through a good marriage to an eligible man. Is it to
spare men from having to take responsibility for anything at
all? To ensure that women are always the accountable ones,
the ones who take the rap? Are men really so incapable of
facing up to responsibility?

No, but the man is in a position of power—he's not
expected to be accountable. The woman is in the posi-

tion of being *haram*: that which is prohibited. As a result, anyone who touches her is touching the whole family unit. It's to touch something forbidden. This prohibition must not be transgressed because women, in such societies, are the warrants of inheritance and clan membership, and they become tantamount to an economic asset. That's why it's essential to know who the father is. And that's the reason for the ban on adultery, otherwise how is the coming child going to inherit? It's all tied up with economic considerations, to such a degree that poets like Abu Nawas came to write:

> *Anifat nafsiya al azizato an taknaa illa bi*
> *koulli shay'en haram.*

(Roughly translated, it means, 'My soul will not be satisfied with anything unless it be forbidden.')

Poets and thinkers were chafing under so many rules and regulations, and began to idealize all that was forbidden. Infringing the prohibitions became a sign of liberation and showed one's repudiation of religious law.

I can think of another reason. I wonder if it's not just as much to do with the fact that oriental families are so fused. Their bodies are merged: a child's body is the property of the parents. So, if a young woman is 'penetrated' outside the extended family framework assigned to her by marriage, it's as if the father were being penetrated by his daughter's lover.

The amalgamation of the family body means that everyone, including the father and mother, feels equally as penetrated as she was!

Yes, they can certainly interpret it as an aggression towards them. The assault on a daughter becomes an assault on all members of the family.

Precisely because of that amalgamation. Although when a girl goes to bed with someone she's attracted to, it can hardly be called an assault! Except where it involves rape, which is different, and I perfectly understand the reaction . . .

[THE FOLLOWING EVENING . . .]

Dad? Shall we start?

Ahlan wa sahlan![3] Off we go.

Why do people need the idea of God? I'm still talking about monotheistic religions, by the way. Why can't a person pick another person to be their 'god', and so on in turn? After all, when you love someone very much he becomes like a 'living god' in your eyes . . . It's like that for me, anyhow; I mean, I'd like to be like that. When I'm in love with a man, I consciously raise him to quasi-divine status. And when we break up it's a painful blow, of course, but sooner or later one always falls in love again, and so I go off in search of another 'god' . . . And in the same way, don't we women become 'goddesses' to our lovers? Or am I being awfully naïve? Is this just a remnant of adolescence that I'm reluctant to let go?

The idea of God was 'invented' to solve the problem of the invisible world and of death. It's a very old idea that was around long before the appearance of monotheistic religions. What happened was that this idea evolved, branching out into multiple forms that varied according to the different peoples and periods concerned. Monotheism, proposing a single god in place of several, was only the latest permutation. As I was saying, it's a notion that seeks to alleviate, or so it claims, man's distress faced with the great unknown, inasmuch as believers are persuaded that there is a 'life' after death. What kind of existence might that be? What becomes of us? Some cultures hit on the idea of heaven, and the fact that we might 'dwell' by God's side after death. Meanwhile there are plenty of people who don't believe in God, who think that mankind is a natural phenomenon, a species on earth like any other, and that after death we merge with nature, we become earth. According to this, the hereafter is nothing but an illusion, born of man's anguished need to explain death, or to understand it. This is not a matter that can be discussed from the standpoint of reason or logic. It can't be criticized rationally, because it springs from the tenets of the heart and the spirit, it's connected to people's fears and weaknesses, to the prospect of death. It deserves to be taken seriously and should not be negated or disparaged, out of respect for the anxieties and obsessions of believers. Out of respect for others, in a word. The only thing you can do when faced with these beliefs, should you feel impelled to make a stand, is to not believe. There are other things you could put your faith in, the individual, for example . . .

So what stops a human being from becoming a kind of 'god' to his fellows?

I'm coming to that. An attempt has been made from within Islam itself. One group began to treat certain people as gods. Its adepts placed all their trust and faith in these figures, and conceptualized their relationship with them. They took such a person to be an instance of divine revelation. He was not himself God, but a reflection of that unknown quantity, the hereafter; for the invisible can only be known or contemplated through the visible. This is how they began deifying flowers, like the rose, or rivers and mountains, in the manner of tribes who believe in several gods. And they also deified human beings.

Do you mean the prophets?

No, prophets only exist in monotheistic religions.

I know, but who were these people through whom others might get a glimpse of the invisible? And I love the idea of the ones who made gods of their flowers, rivers and mountains! I love it!

I'm not sure we have the right to talk about them, especially as most Muslims view them as non-believers, renegades, apostates and infidels. They suffered much persecution and oppression as a result. That's why it's best to respect them by not discussing them . . .

How do you mean, 'not sure we have the right'?

It's very difficult to talk about . . . You see, there were groups who believed that God manifested Himself in Ali, but, to avoid misunderstanding (because a man who is born, falls sick, eats and dies like a common mortal cannot be regarded as God, or that's what these believers hold; God cannot die, and therefore one has to create an image of God which has no human counterpart), then, these groups came up with the following compromise: we will base ourselves, they said, upon Ali as a symbol, rather than upon his image as a human being, conditioned by birth and death. But this idea was rejected by the majority of Muslims. The various Sufi schools profess this kind of belief in ordinary mortals. In effect they transposed *al-wataniyya*, the belief in multiple deities, from things onto humans, onto man.

But a person can be a god, not of course in the religious sense – like Jesus, who performed miracles, walked on water and was resurrected – but more in the sense of a 'guide', as in Buddhism. The Buddha was a man who attained a kind of perfection . . .

Yes, that can exist, and Buddhism is proof of that. I was offering examples from within monotheistic religions. But there's Buddhism, of course there is, and there's also the figure of the guru who is looked up to as a master, as one who has arrived at a certain truth, as one who 'knows'. His disciples listen to him and obey him as though his word proceeded from God. This is another experience of life that should be respected and not judged, and discussed in a reasonable way, because truth flows from more than just one source.

If some people have managed to live without the idea of God, and a few, like the Buddha, have reached truth and perfection on earth, why do others still feel the need for something more? With the knowledge – I realize it now, talking to you – that if ordinary men came to be regarded as gods, it could lead to disaster! Think of the loony sects that preach the end of the world or extra-terrestrial landings or compulsory collective suicide and whathaveyou. Not to mention the dictators who claim godlike attributes for themselves; there are more than a few of those!

Yes, it's an idea that has seeped into politics. Many presidents, many leaders around the world are thought by their followers to be perfect paragons among men.

So if there has to be one leader over all, let him be from nowhere, at least!

But believers have a tendency to transpose this habit of hierarchy onto earthly powers. As soon as a man is treated as a god, it's all too easy for him to command the obedience of others. It could be argued that monotheism paved the way for the invention of dicta-torships . . . These simply displaced the idea of a sin-gle god onto that of the single dictator, the inspired chief, et cetera.

Or onto a bunch of mini-dictatorships, as in Arab-Muslim countries, where the smallest sheikh can issue a fatwa on a whim, against whatever he likes, and the people go along with it. But have any philosophers ever looked into the fact that man can be a god to himself? That he carries his own heaven and hell inside? Why can't one be one's own god, or one's own demon?

There are certainly people who think along those lines. Everything pertaining to the realm of things outside the real becomes a strictly personal affair. Such as love, for example. Each of us loves the one he pleases and conceives of love as he sees fit, and practices love by his own rules. Such ideas exist, they have been posit-ed, but they count among the most complex of philo-sophical puzzles. These are questions that came into existence with humanity, questions to which there is no single answer. We have to accept the multiplicity of viewpoints and opinions. And this is why it's so potentially dangerous to bring faith into the political arena: faith then becomes an obligation for all, and yet not all of us believe in the same things. Christianity settled the question as follows: you want to believe, you believe, you go to Church and you pray. In soci-eties that have lost their religious faith, civil codes apply, with universal jurisdiction, but these laws are not concerned with personal creeds. Beliefs or faith become the exclusive business of the person who professes them, and must absolutely never be imposed on someone who lacks faith, or doesn't want it.

The separation of Church and State was a salutary measure, therefore. And here precisely lies the problem with Islam: the Muslims refuse to effect this separation. Hence, the despotic character of their religion. Islam seeks to foist its laws on everyone. And if you're a Muslim who happens to want to change your religion, well, you can't do it, it's not allowed (it's known as *al-ridda*). Anyone who commits this sin becomes a renegade who may be executed with impunity. This to my mind is one of Islam's most serious drawbacks: it has turned into a coercive doctrine. A significant proportion of Muslims no longer believes, but has to pretend that it does and submit to the diktats of the faith—especially if it is in a state that has adopted that faith for its Law. So we can see a kind of fissure within the societies of the Muslim world, to the extent that this ideology is no longer commensurate with the needs of the people and has to be imposed by force. As a result, most people are obeying rules they've ceased to believe in. This leads to considerable tensions and disturbances in mixed societies such as Lebanon, Iraq or Egypt, which harbour various non-Islamic religions.

Before it gets to that point, it might be a good thing if they tried reading the Koran in their native languages, and weren't forced to learn Arabic. Maybe that way they'd get a clearer idea of what it is they're supposed to be reading and believing!

It would make no difference to the dogma or the ideology . . . They only insist on Arabic for the call to prayer. In Turkey, for instance, they read the Koran in Turkish. Everyone can read it in their own language.

But learning Arabic is compulsory. It is in Iran.

Not everyone speaks Arabic . . .

Not everyone perhaps, but anyone who wants to study theology.

That's right. You can't learn the Koran unless you speak Arabic.

Well then, why don't they translate the Koran into every language?

They do. You can get it in Indonesian, in Urdu, in Turkish. But if someone wants to study Arabic, you can't tell him not to. All the most committed students learn Arabic. For them, the specificity of Islam resides in the Arab tongue. They prefer to read the Koran as it was dictated to the Prophet, in its original form. They feel that their faith is incomplete if they don't read it in Arabic, the language in which it was revealed.

Islamists claim that the Koran improved the situation of women because, before Islam came along, female infants were

4 Name given under
Islam to the period
that preceded it. The
word means 'igno-
rance' in Arabic.

*buried at birth. Is that true? At the same time I've always
wondered how the Al-Jahiliyya[4] poets, who wrote so lyrically
of love and women, could bear to live in a society where the
most hideous crime was perpetrated, the murder of babies at
birth simply because they fell into an 'inferior category' . . .*

I don't think there's any truth to those stories. It's an
invention of Muslim historians, this yarn about pre-
Islamic Arabs burying baby girls alive. There is not the
slightest evidence to prove that the Arabs buried
their daughters, for fear of poverty or dishonour. We
should take all such tales with a pinch of salt. The very
fact of calling the pre-Islamic period a dark age of
Jahiliyya is a mistake that needs correcting. In reality,
these pre-Islamic Arabs were a cultured race that produced a thought and a civilization. There are no
grounds for calling this Jahiliyya, it's all wrong. We
should refuse to employ the word. Not only this, all
the theories or alleged facts about that period should
be revised and indeed discredited.

*Because as soon as one gets into the amatory and erotic verse
of those days, the way it lingers over love, women, sexuality,
it seems extraordinary that —*

Even more, look at what they had to say about female
autonomy! Women were the ones who initiated
divorce proceedings, women decided whether they
wanted to get married, and to whom . . . There are stories about one woman who is said to have married
forty men! And no one thought badly of her.

Was it a matriarchal society?

No, but women enjoyed considerable freedom, and in certain tribes —

They were pagans, weren't they?

Yes.

And most of their deities were female?

Yes, for example they had Al-Uzza, Manat and Al-Lat.[5]

5 The triple goddesses of the pre-Islamic pantheon.

Muslims accuse this culture of burying its daughters alive at birth, but I think women are still being buried alive at birth today . . . All through their childhood and adolescence, their heads are being shoved under water. They're told, they're made to believe, that the fault is inherently theirs and that their body doesn't belong to them, it's the property of the father, the mother, the family in general or the rest of the society around them. They're told that having their period makes them impure and debars them from joining with the community to pray or to fast; it makes them unfit to touch the Koran or even to be in the same room as a sheikh. Their virginity is supposed to be the seal of their integrity and reputation — and of the family's reputation, of course, not to say that of the whole village! And so we get honour killings and all that. It doesn't make me feel any better to know that honour killings are known to happen in southern Italy, in Corsica, in the south of Spain, in Portugal, in all sorts of rural communities. Just because there was a time in Europe when men behaved like barbarians towards women doesn't make everything relative! Women's second-class status compared to men in every circumstance; the fact that it takes two women to testify against one man . . . Even the dowry given to a girl is a two-edged advantage, I think, most obviously because it turns her into a commodity to be 'bought', but also because it removes any incentive to pursue financial independence.

The claim that Islam liberated women, especially in the light of its Law and general principles, is a very questionable message which should be revised wholesale.

How can you possibly be 'liberating' women when at the same time you're putting them down from earliest childhood, making them feel inferior to men, telling them they're impure when they have a period and demanding two female witnesses to balance the testimony of any one man? It's got to stop!

Yes, the testimony of a man is worth that of two women.

It's the limit, isn't it?

And on top of that a daughter inherits only half of what a son receives!

The submissiveness drummed into women under Islam gives rise to strange phenomena like the 'headscarf attitude', which I see as comparable to the 'punk attitude'. It's about adopting an extreme attitude and making an identity of it . . . That way you can test your resistance to the outside world, sound out the limits of other people and whip up a 'cause'. Suddenly you exist, because you're defending 'your skin'. This skin can be represented by the veil as much as by body piercings, leather gear, mohican crests, army fatigues or whatever. The headscarf turns into a rallying cry, a mark of identity. These girls are shackling themselves, often voluntarily, with the chains already prepared for them! It's nuts! They create prohibitions for themselves, they're used to it, and it's not an easy habit to drop. The problem is that these dress codes are taken for the expression of divine will, which makes them extra-loaded and dangerous. Because there's no room for the least opening, for any dialogue or rebellion. It must be really hard for a girl to bare her head after years of wearing a scarf, and in such a closed, tradition-ridden environment. Do you think Islam can ever be modernized? Who could make that happen?

The obstacle here is the way in which the Koran is read. A text is defined by its interpretation. So when you analyse the relationship between Koranic scripture and society over the last fifteen hundred years, you find that all sorts of shifts have taken place. At the outset, Islam was a 'tolerant' religion. Under the Abbasid dynasty, homosexuality was admitted and accepted and it was natural to report, 'So-and-so arrived with his *ghulam*[6] . . .' Speaking of which, I saw in yesterday's paper that a court in Massachusetts has legalized gay marriage.

Hurray! Good for them!

Homosexuality used to be perfectly ordinary and common in Arab society. And so, if the text exists in and

6 A youth, the paramour of an older man.

through the readings that are made of it, Muslim society can certainly be modernized. If ever an outward-looking, progressive political system were to grant people the freedom to think for themselves and to interpret religious texts in the light of the present, in the light of the problems that currently beset mankind, in the light of life as it is lived, then the Koran could certainly be updated. A scripture must after all be as mobile as life itself, since it was revealed to assist mankind and to serve society, not to be served by it. Religion is made for man, it's there to enhance his freedom and nurture his development, not to hold him back. If we accept this, it follows that religious texts should be read from the perspective of human needs, taking account of the problems faced by mankind at any one time.

And who's to decide that? The sheikhs?

No! The man on the street! If political authority were itself free, and guaranteed individual freedoms, then the citizens who are not religious would be entitled to express an opinion on the subject of those who are. If there was more freedom, most people would concur in explaining the texts in a way that accords with human needs and lives. Therefore I think that the main obstacle is political: political power is always on the side of religion.

Really?

I mean that the ruling power is not impartial, like an umpire, but it's a player on the 'other team'. If they'd had the freedom, Arab societies would have been able to develop. There are isolated examples: President Bourguiba granted considerable rights to Tunisian women. Many believers protested that this went against the faith. Even so, the new rights were put to the vote and passed. The King of Morocco, Mohammed VI, has just now put forward bills that would emancipate Moroccan women on several levels, and this despite the religious lobby's conservative reading of the Koran. This shows that the main brake on progress comes from the top. The ruler should be a moderator, not an active participant in the debate. The authorities should underwrite the space of freedom in which dialogue and democratic discussion can flourish. When that happens, religious texts will be interpreted in accordance with real life and its problems. Because, at times of historical transition, God himself, who revealed certain *ayat* or verses, saw fit to replace them with more appropriate sayings. Man could 'imitate' God, then, and move on from this blinkered, inflexible reading of the Koran. Many verses which had once been revealed began to appear unworkable, later on . . . So God replaced them with new ones, and dictated a verse to justify this:

> *Ma nansakh min ayaten aw monsiha, na'ti bi kheiren minha aw mithliha.*[7]

7 'Whatever a Verse (revelation) do We abrogate or cause to be forgotten, We bring a better one or similar to it.' Surah 2, v. 106. *The Noble Qur'an*, King Fahd Complex for the Printing of the Noble Qur'an, Madinah, K.S.A., 2006.

Thus it seems that God updated his laws, as expressed in the *ayat*, whenever they ceased to correspond with reality. And in fact his example is one to be followed. People could adjust their reading of revealed scripture in much the same way, and recast the text to suit their needs.

But some would object that if that were allowed, anybody could change the law on a whim . . .

Of course, there would have to be strict rules governing the process.

Do you think religions can withstand the march of science? There are more and more discoveries threatening religious certainties, aren't there? It's in the interest of all religions to open up and to adapt . . . And yet the effect seems to be the opposite, as though they became even more hard line as a reaction. In this day and age I think it's a crime, for instance, to forbid the use of condoms on religious grounds. It's nothing to do with science, it's a social issue . . .

It's a question of faith. According to some believers, there's no scientific discovery that was not anticipated by the Koran.

Yes, I know!

So what is one to say to that? I could show you an essay written by a fervent Muslim in which he contends that the events of 9/11 had already been announced by God!

Who wrote that?

A fundamentalist! Someone sent it on to me. It rests upon the most absurdly elaborate calculations!

. . . ?

There will always be people eager to naysay science, or to proclaim that science itself is dealt with in the Koran, along with every new discovery . . .

However, I don't think the religious text will be able to hold out for ever. It's too far removed from the world, too disconnected from reality. I repeat, the Koran can only resist as it does by dint of faith, not reason.

You said once that Islam denies free will, or Islam is against individual freedom, do you remember? You demonstrated your thesis, but I can't remember how it went now. Was it something to do with the Islamic ban on changing one's religion?

I was making the point that Islam has no concept of the 'individual' as a free and independent agent; it ties him down by subordinating him to the community, the '*umma*-nation'. *Umma* is the central element in Islam's social philosophy, and takes precedence over the individual. As a result the individual finds his freedom negated in every sphere. Personal freedom is curtailed by the rules and values imposed by the *umma*, its religion and its culture. There is a traditional saying that encapsulates this: '*Man qal fi ddini bira'yihi, fa houwa mokhti'on, wa law assab.'* That is, 'he who advises on religion with reference to his own lights and reason will be at fault, even if his reasoning is sound.'

And therefore the only view will be that of the collective, the *umma*'s version, never the individual's!

The Arab world has become completely schizophrenic, torn between its fascination with the West and the hatred it feels for that same culture.

As I told you before, this kind of society — typified by lack of freedom — divides itself into two cultural levels. One is the visible level that corresponds to the majority of believers, together with the political system; the other is masked, hidden from view. It's the hidden level that attracts the people who want to conduct their lives more freely. This is clearly a form of hypocrisy, of a split personality . . .

Obviously!

But schizophrenia is something else, it's a clinical condition, whereas here we're talking about people who have two facets, or faces. One face prays, fasts and hands over the *zakat*,[8] while the other defies every prohibition, for example by indulging in boundless sexual licence. These people practise all that is *halal*, or permitted, in the visible circles of society while slipping underground to practice all that is *haram*.

But how on earth do they do it?

8 Religious tax collected on behalf of the poor.

It's basically due to the absence of liberties. People are forced to exercise their freedom in secret.

I just wonder how anyone can stand to live in those conditions? Having to lie about everything . . .

It's terrible, but they manage to come up with alternative stratagems.

How?

Every human being is obliged to invent cunning ploys so as to exercise his freedom, even within his own home. To avoid falling foul of religious edicts . . .

We all need to keep a part of ourselves secret . . . It's what we do as adolescents when we want to construct a different personality, unlike that of our parents, and assert our own private experience. A teenager is testing her parents' limits and her own limits at the same time . . . But once past that stage, you've got to take responsibility for your actions. You can't play hide-and-seek for ever, because sooner or later those underhand pleasures, exciting as they are, begin to degenerate into something rather 'grubby' which musn't come to light and must absolutely never be aired. It'd cause too many tensions and dramas.

[LATER . . .]

If religious fanatics acknowledged their desires, wouldn't they become a bit more level-headed? The trouble is, they can't face up to them.

That's true, but being dishonest with oneself and telling lies is not the sole preserve of religious people . . . You'll find people telling lies even when they live in a more permissive environment. Like a woman who continues to deceive her husband instead of simply saying, 'I don't love you any more!' Or a son who can't come clean with his father, and declare: 'I'm in love with this girl, or this boy.' As you rightly pointed out, we have a propensity to exalt the forbidden. People like getting up to things in secret . . . So what's to be done? It's not only a religious problem, it has a bearing on social behaviour.

Yes, but it adulterates the value of things. Something quite beautiful becomes 'unhealthy' or 'shabby' if it's done in a hole-and-corner way for too long. I'm not saying that we've got to do everything in broad daylight in front of the whole world. I love the forbidden, the things we get up to in secret . . . I'm talking about more straightforward issues like sex outside marriage, for instance. In some places, especially in Arab-Muslim societies, this act is reviled as being the work of Satan himself!

In Europe, the only constraint you might want to kick against is the law, but you're not having to run away from religion, or the prying eyes of society. Here you can love whoever you want, the way you want. There may be people who have it in for you, who object to your choices or your tastes, but there are others who will stand up for you and maybe even share the same tastes. Here you are free to cre-ate a secret or parallel life out of coquetry or playfulness or in pursuit of the most absolute bliss . . . It's not a matter of life and death, as it is in the Arab world today!

This penchant for a hidden life is a social phenomenon, and it's not confined to the most observant believers, or even to Muslims. It has to do with human nature, and not only with religion . . . However, it may well be exacerbated by religion.

Let's say that religion exacerbates frustration. Men are sexually frustrated in the Arab world—you can see it in the way they look at you! So they get what they can, but sneakily, of course.

Of course! It's a mendacious society. Hypocritical.

That's what I'm trying to say! There's the most incredible violence, at least against girls . . . A girl walking down the street, if she looks the least bit sexy she becomes the target of an absolute verbal lynching! Words hurled at her like stones! I can't stand it, it makes me want to chop their ends off! (Laughter.)

But look at Beirut, or Damascus—

Exactly, look at them!

Never mind the bigotry—there's still a 'secret society' that thrives unseen, the underside of the visible society.

I want to insist on this business of frustration. The more frustrated people are, the more they cling to the most hard-line religions, or to the traditions that keep them so frustrated. Any woman who has the guts to express her sexuality normally is treated as a whore. I had men friends in Beirut who'd tell me all about some girl they 'loved'. So I'd say, 'Great, isn't it wonderful to make love when you're mad about each other?' and they'd go, 'Oh no, I couldn't go to bed with her, I love her!'

You're inclined to see things from a psychoanalytic angle. It's possible, I suppose.

I think that if the Islamists in Pakistan or Afghanistan — Taliban types — or the ones who live in the most pious quarters of Damascus and Riyadh, in Saudi Arabia—

They're frustrated.

Absolutely! I'm sure that if all those frustrated men entertained a normal relationship with women, if they were able to make love, and fall in love, and gaze at their own bodies, and enfold the body of a woman, then they'd be less stupid and narrow-minded and, above all, less dangerous! Without wanting to sound like a hippie, because I'm not 'right-on' at all, I do think that if all those fanatics had the capacity to love in the widest sense of the word, their minds and bodies could never have been so Talibanized . . .

They're not only frustrated in relation to women, but also in terms of their everyday lives. They have nothing to do, nothing to aim for. This may well give rise to a delirious despair that drives them to embrace religious causes.

Lots of aspects of religion seem to demand a psychological explanation, in my opinion.

I must say, I agree with you there. A person whose social or sexual life is a failure, who is incapable of communicating with others, who doesn't create and who has nothing to say, is inevitably going to flounder. He makes up for his inadequacies by plunging into any cause that makes him feel alive, and, more importantly, useful. And religion is simply the most effective and potent refuge for such men, especially in the Arab world.

Yes, it gives them this feeling of supreme power . . .

Which goes to show that such characters don't have a thought in their heads, they're thoroughly ignorant. They parrot the teachings . . . mindlessly . . . They build up an enemy for themselves in order to brandish their power, their 'new feeling of being alive', because without an antagonist they'd be left high and dry! They are not satisfied with having faith—they've got to wield that faith against someone.

I see them swanning about Paris, these youths who fancy themselves as up-and-coming imams or precocious theology students, wearing their djellabas over their Nikes, with little beards and white skullcaps . . . I'm probably caricaturing them unfairly, but I tell you, at close quarters, there's not a decent looker among the lot of them!

171

A boy their age would normally be passionate about sports, college, girls, his mates . . . I find it tragic to see them devote themselves to the service of a travesty of religion, giving themselves over to ugliness, frustration and death, instead of opening up to the world and to other people!

Stairway to Heaven
(LED ZEPPELIN, 1971)

NINAR: *What's your relationship with religion?*

ADONIS: Although I was brought up in a religious household, and had immense love for my father, I have no relationship with religion. None whatsoever.

What about the Alawites? Do you feel Alawite? Is it important to you?

Not at all. If I have any link to the Alawites, it would be chiefly social and historical. Actually I feel great sympathy towards them, as a people that has been constantly hounded, banished, martyred and decimated, throughout its history . . . My heart goes out to such a wretched and excluded tribe. I'm reminded of Bergson, who was Jewish by birth but decided to convert to Christianity and be baptized a Catholic; and then, with the rise of Nazism and the growing persecution of the Jews, he felt a solidarity with them and changed his mind about becoming a Catholic. This wasn't for religious reasons, it was a way of making a stand, it was an ethical act . . .

My attitude to the Alawites is ethical in much the same way, perhaps. I was born a member of that community and, although I don't hold with religion of any sort, I respect believers because I respect human beings. I respect their freedom.

I hope it won't upset you if I say that they are a medieval sect that treats women with blatant contempt! I'm not thinking of politics when I say that . . . I'm referring to the Alawite 'religion' separately from their leadership in Syria.

I would have preferred to hear an opinion grounded in some knowledge of the subject, some life experience amongst these people, rather than in a kind of patronizing dismissiveness . . .

I don't have a problem with religions or religious people, they can worship a cockroach for all I care, it's the least of my worries. I just want them to keep out of my way and leave me in peace . . . I'm only repeating what I've heard you say, you and Arwad, on the plight of women, and that's a subject that does interest me.

There are so many rumours and tall tales about them, you know, you should be a bit careful. For example, Alawite women are under no obligation to wear the veil, and they never do. On the other hand, they are denied the right to religious instruction.

I know.

But there are many others who are not taught about the faith either.

Men, do you mean?

Yes, men. For example, the majority of Alawites are not initiated into what they call the Secrets and the 'Ultimate Knowledge'. It's not only women who are kept out . . . And Alawite women are pretty well integrated into everyday life. That's saying something, when you compare with Arab societies!

If you like. Suddenly, their condition strikes me as downright idyllic! But maybe I should check with a woman about that! (Laughter.)

Okay, so it's not all bad. One of the few things I like about the Muslim religion is that it doesn't foster guilt feelings about sex or money . . .

Yes, where that's concerned man has a direct line to God through his faith. There is no intermediary, no priest, and therefore no feeling of guilt.

On the other hand, what I find thoroughly stupid is that everything is 'written', and the ultimate goal of life is to prepare for one's entrance to Paradise. It implies that there can be no joy here on earth — the only joy is stored up in heaven. Which makes it a gamble at best, and a swindle as far as I'm concerned! The belief that joy and happiness are rewards that can only be claimed in heaven provides an excuse not to improve everyday conditions down here, it discourages one from protesting, from dreaming, from creating. It seems to me that even Buddhism is somewhat defeatist, because it preaches that if you've been dealt an unfair hand in life and you're struggling to get by, it's the fault of your karma. So when you find yourself in a difficult or tragic situation, you're somehow already the victim of your bad karma, and paying for it.

They live in hiding, in secret . . .

Yes, but some people don't live at all.

It takes a certain affluence to indulge one's pleasures and desires.

You're not suggesting it comes down to money?

Of course it does! Some people can't afford to treat a woman to a cup of coffee! They can't afford to travel, or buy anything for themselves . . .

But pleasure begins when one is honest with oneself, and happy with one's body.

Pleasure is a kind of luxury.

What do you understand by 'luxury'?

Luxury is every want that comes after the satisfaction of essential needs like food and clothing. And there are people who lack even that bare minimum.

Don't tell me you've got to be flush before you can love!

Well, first you must feel convinced about it.

I would have thought so!

And then, once you're convinced, you must have the wherewithal to act on your convictions.

Not in every situation . . .

Almost all.

I don't agree . . .

Some people can't even stretch to buying a bottle of wine! Anyhow, these are variables that depend on the circumstances in each case. We're generalizing.

But we don't need a statistical breakdown! Of course we're generalizing, but can't we still ask ourselves that kind of question?

You're dispensing judgements and opinions that can't be reached so easily. One has to live in a place and know it firsthand, to gain any insight into how people go about their lives . . . You see, my darling, it's important to be precise about these things. You can't be laying down the law about people just like that.

Well, I do have male friends in Beirut and I know what their life is like. They're the same age as me and they want to have a good time, so they pick up prostitutes — it's the best they can do! Which is to say that prohibitions do exist, and do have a crushing effect on society. I don't mind them going to prostitutes, I'm querying the fact that it's their only option.

All the more reason!

There's no absolute need to be rich in order to experience excitement or adventure, it's more a question of attitude.

Let's admit this attitude exists; we need go no further than Ras Beirut to see it in action. But if you visit Bourj Hammoud or Hay Elleja,[1] you find yourself wondering how the people who live there manage to enjoy themselves and fulfil their desires. Economic hardship and unemployment have a lot to do with it.

That's terrible, what you're saying! It makes out that pleasures are a luxury, a privilege of the wealthy or the middle classes! That's terrible! I always thought that fun and pleasure were entirely a matter of disposition or desire (as in, 'I want to feel pleasure' or 'I accept to feel pleasure'). I never imagined it was a social perk! When pleasure is such a subjective, personal thing . . . Of course, if everyone is out to enjoy the same thrills, taking their cue from the pleasure of others and copying it, then yes, you'd need money to purchase the pleasures you envy in other people. Like going on holiday to the same resort as the neighbours or buying the same car as your best friend or giving your wife the same sort of jewellery as your boss gave to his or going out with a busty blonde just because the trendiest top models are blondes — that sort of thing. Highly expensive for sure, but that's not pleasure as I see it — that's living by proxy. It's

[1] Three celebrated neighbourhoods in Beirut. The first is an upmarket district, the other two are working-class.

like the audience at a bullfight — they seem to be wanting to share in the bullfighter's courage, only vicariously. To put it more crudely, they want to borrow someone else's balls. I've come around at last to understanding the duel between bull and man. I can accept it because the matador takes risks; his life is on the line, he can get seriously hurt. I've grown to respect the passionate encounter between beast and man, but I can't stomach those vultures looking on, they're nothing but cowardly voyeurs. As though a crowd of people in need of an orgasm had surrounded a captive couple making love, just so as to experience a vicarious climax. Let all those peeping toms go down into the ring themselves, let them face the bull, then we'd be talking . . .

It's true that pleasure is individual so long as it remains confined to the individual concerned. But does such a pleasure actually exist? No, because pleasure requires a partner, an other. And the search for this partner or this other leads us into the social domain, with its values, traditions and standards of living. In that sense pleasure is a function of society and of the conditions in a particular society. And from that point on, we have to concede that pleasure in today's world is bought and sold like any other commodity.

I agree with you that pleasure calls for the other, or an other. That's why I find it hard to understand people whose pleasure is mainly focused on masturbation. It's fine if it's just from time to time . . . But personally, I need a partner in order to feel pleasure and to share it.

[ANOTHER DAY . . .]

What do you think about 'suicide' in the context of resist-
ance? Whether it's kamikaze pilots or Islamic jihadists. I'm
aware that in the Koran, jihad doesn't translate as killing
oneself. Jihad means something else. But of course I'm all for
the resistance to dictatorships, occupying armies, tyrants
and such. I'm positively fascinated by this concept and,
when I was small, I wanted to join in the resistance, during
the Lebanese war for example, especially when the Israeli
army invaded us in 1982.

I was eleven years old, I was in sixth grade. The inva-
sion began on 6 June 1982, I believe. The Israeli air force was
bombing the south, I could hear the planes over Beirut, it
was three or four in the afternoon, and you and Mum were
over at the University teaching your classes . . . I had got
home from school by then, and I'd already had my lunch.

I felt scared because I could tell that the noise of these
planes – the racket that was so familiar to me and to every
person in Lebanon – sounded different this time. It was
more than just a few aircraft having fun with the sound bar-
rier over our heads in order to tear our nerves to shreds. The
noise went on longer this time, and was punctuated by the
thudding of shells. All of a sudden a hail of Kalashnikov fire
came down right, left and centre and an invisible wave of
gooseflesh swept over the living matter of the city.
Everything stood transfixed: buildings, stones, plants,
birds, cats, dogs, people, tables, chairs, cars, sand . . . Even

the sea, I'm quite sure, shivered and shrank back to protect
its inhabitants.

This ushered in a new phase of violence, nothing like
the civil war which was so foul, stupid and unforgiveable.
Now, suddenly, the enemy was different, mightier and more
mysterious, it attacked from sea, land and sky. And when it
came from the sky . . . there was no escape, we were like lab-
oratory mice who don't know where the hand will swoop
down from next to inject them. It was an astounding experience for me, and I'm glad I stayed in Beirut and that by
staying, I resisted. It was a new experience too, with different sounds (because the Israeli army had these modern products or rather weapons, brand new ordnance, latest models,
things that the dated old Lebanese militia didn't have, they
were totally behind the times!). New noises that sounded
surreal to my ears! I've never heard anything like it since,
not even in the best American sci-fi movies! Plus the
weapons had new names: cluster bombs, pressurized bombs,
phosphus bombs . . .

It was the period of surprise raids, and sham raids, and
cats mewing in the rubble, and hundreds of budgies set loose
by their owners . . . But as the birds had been born in cap-
tivity, they weren't very good at flying or finding their own
food. To free them was only an indirect way of killing them
. . .

For the first time ever we had to leave our flat and move
to a safer part of Beirut, staying with people, which meant

saying goodbye to neighbours and childhood playmates, because everyone was dispersing to seek refuge wherever they could. We also had to leave our pets behind . . . I had to give away my first cat, Blanchette, a wild creature with tall ears like those of a fox. Because I couldn't take her where we were going, especially as if we had to flee at short notice, we couldn't bring her along. So she was given to someone who took her to the country. For me, aged eleven, it was a very sad moment, mixed up with a sense of unfairness and an overwhelming guilt!

We remained in the city besieged by Israeli forces for two months, under the most unimaginable bombardment (a thousand shells per hour!). The fighters put up a heroic resistance to save Beirut from falling into Israeli hands. Then one day the army marched in. Beirut had fallen.

After horribly violent street battles (we spent practically all of our time in the shelters), the Israeli army gained control of Beirut and dug itself in.

So now we could see the enemy's face for the first time. They looked like ordinary men kitted out in a total 'it's off to war we go' look, with bulging backpacks, a radio for keeping in touch, netted helmets, camouflage khakis, the lot. They patrolled the city in this get-up, ten by ten. They moved without making a sound, so that you could turn a corner and run slap into them without warning — and get the fright of your life!

One day the army decided to pull out. I was with Mother that morning on the main shopping street of West Beirut, in Hamra, and we saw this Israeli soldier standing up in a jeep with a megaphone, declaiming in Arabic: 'People of Beirut, stop attacking us, we are planning to withdraw!' It was out of this world! The Israelis left Beirut at the end of September 1982. But they remained in Lebanon for a long time, especially in the south, and so the attacks on the army and its collaborators were stepped up. In 1984, I think, there was a 'first', a crazy incident I could hardly believe, the first suicide bombing, when Sanaa Mehaidleh blew herself up in the middle of an Israeli convoy in south Lebanon. She had belonged to a secular party. It made a huge impression on me. I couldn't get my mind around it. Of course, I'd heard of the Japanese kamikazes during the Second World War who used to slam their planes into American targets. But the same thing was now happening on my territory, in my country . . . And this was a woman, a young woman, who had gone for the army rather than for civilians, and without any religious axe to grind . . .

To become an anonymous hero is a vocation requiring enormous passion and generosity. Perhaps a touch of madness, as well . . . Think of the American Indians resisting the white settlers, or the French Resistance during the Second World War . . . I would support an intelligent choice of targets, always maintaining a respect for innocent and civilian lives. For instance, it would be okay to attack elements of civil infrastructure such as banks or bridges or the railway network. Or military infrastructures, such as arms factories or supply depots. But it's wrong to go for innocent civilians, I think, whatever the cause you're fighting for. It's a criminal thing to do. Just because the enemy displays an indiscriminate brutality doesn't mean you should do the same. If the only retort you can make to injustice is death, you've merely justified that injustice by not acting intelligently, by refusing to think about the shape of the future or to build a political project. It's saying no to life, in a sense . . . while operating on the same vile level as the 'enemy', whoever it may be.

That's why I loved Elia Suleiman's film, Divine Intervention: *the tone is perfectly judged, subtle and clever. The resistance is depicted with humour and, most importantly, a hefty dose of self-criticism — that's crucial! The film is true to life, which is why it's so effective. And also why it went down badly with the Arab audience, who are used to movies that drone on about victimhood and feature lots of women-in-traditional-dress-weeping-in-the-olive-groves. More recently, I also enjoyed the documentary by Eyal Sivan[2] and Michel Khleifé,[3]* Route 180. *It needs no comment from me, as the testimonies it contains speak for themselves . . . The most moving part comes at the end, in the last scene. Here we see a resistance worth its salt in that it urges people towards life, not death. The film tells whole generations of young people that they do have a choice, that there's another way of hitting back or resisting that doesn't involve blowing oneself up. Easy for me to say, of course. I'm not in the position of a young Palestinian in the occu-*

2 Eyal Sivan (b. 1964): Israeli film director, born in Haifa.

3 Michel Khleifé (b. 1950): Palestinian film director, born in Nazareth.

pied territories, with no opportunity to see such films, no leisure to step back for a moment and reflect, whose only source of information is Al-Jazeera . . . If the Arab networks would only fulfil their cultural responsibilities by showing that kind of film, instead of historical made-for-TV dramas glorifying Islam and the Arabs or American sitcoms that encourage viewers to consume rather than to reflect, it would be a small step in the right direction . . .

Anyway, here's something that I find simultaneously violent and romantic: whenever a suicide bombing is reported anywhere in the world, I always wonder whether bits of the bomber were recovered and what they did with them . . . I think to myself: this is crazy, here's this man who wanted to murder scores of people but the amazing thing is how at the moment of the explosion, a ghastly fusion takes place between his body and those of his victims! Their bodies end up mangled together, their bits and pieces all combined, their blood mixed into one pool. Like a macabre orgy! In the final instance, it seems to me, the suicide bomber's intention is obliterated by this climactic union with his victims . . . Like a 'kiss of death', somehow . . .

That's very nicely put. And I agree with you, violence is only excusable when it's a case of resisting occupation.

Hold on, I'm not saying that I defend suicide bombing!

I'm in favour of resistance to aggression, invasion or occupation, and I also accept that there can be no resistance without violence. Other than these exceptional cases, however, I am absolutely against all forms of violence. Because if I'm unable to sway others by means of my ideas, my actions or my work, I shall certainly not succeed with the methods of the sword, with imprisonment, oppression or expulsion. My philosophy on this lies closer to Gandhi's.

Oh, yes! What an impressive man . . . Knowing about his story has helped me hugely in my own life. To me, he's the strongest man who ever lived in the history of humanity, because he fought against man's so-called natural tendency to violence!

Absolutely! I condemn all struggles that are founded on violence. There's no excuse for them, ever . . . But what you said before was very fine and right. Under an occupation there's no alternative but to fight back, to defend those you love, because all occupation is a humiliation. It becomes a duty to defend one's honour, along with one's family and home . . .

Much as I respect Gandhi, though, I'd still support the use of violence against military targets. That's why I admire the 'refuseniks' (lots of Israeli soldiers have deserted, which takes incredible bravery!). In spite of all the punishments they were risking, they refused to carry out orders. It shows that the soldiers in the occupied territories have a choice, to obey orders or to desert . . . And once they've chosen to stay, I reckon they constitute legitimate targets, because they've made the choice, it's their job.

In other words, a resistance should focus primarily
upon military objectives . . .

Yes, military and political. If you want to paralyse a coun-
try, there's no point in attacking buses, schools or places of
worship. You've got to blow up the banks and the bridges!

And the installations that shield the military.

Still on the subject of religion, but on a more cheerful and
aesthetic note: the characters that attract me most in the his-
tory of monotheism are, first of all, St Francis of Assisi,
because he had such a wonderful rapport with animals, and
secondly — for the image of him — St Simon Stylites. This
man spent twenty years on top of a column, sixty feet above
the ground! I've been to the place where the base of his col-
umn is supposedly still standing, at Aleppo in Syria. What
a crackpot genius he must have been! What an idea, to camp
out on top of a column! It's an art performance in the con-
temporary sense, but it's also an amazing symbol of virility,
like keeping an erection up for twenty years! But the eroti-
cism of the gesture is directed, in its extreme tension,
towards God as much as towards man . . . What do you
make of this unbelievable character? Were there any crazed
eccentrics in Islamic history?

He was certainly a most unusual fellow, and I agree
with the way you perceive him. Islam can offer some
similar oddities, although none on a column, I'm
afraid. There's Al-Hallaj,[4] or the notable Rabi'a al-

4 Al-Hallaj (?–922):
poet and one of the
greatest of Arab-
Muslim mystics.
Accused of betraying
the faith, he was cruci-
fied, mutilated and
burned.

189

5 Rabi'a al-Adawiyya
(?–752): Arab-Muslim
poet famed for intro-
ducing the idea of
divine love into Arab
mysticism.

Adawiyya.[5] The latter was a poet who addressed God in her writings as though he were her lover!

Both those you've mentioned are pet favourites of mine, I adore them. They were geniuses in the way they saw the world through the sublimity of their verse . . .

Heroes

(DAVID BOWIE, 1977)

NINAR: *I want to come back to the question people are always asking me: 'What did you learn from your father?' I think it's time for me to take stock. Time to assess what I've seen and learned through you, in order to begin to exploit it and 'make it my own'. I guess the reason I could never bring myself to spell out clearly what it was that I'd learned is that I wanted to keep a large space open for you in my life. I needed to need you! My expectation of a reaction from you was what gave me the illusion of your presence. But if I begin to put together and use the things I've learned from you, it'll mean that I am gradually accepting our separation and the fact that I'm grown up. I hated books when I was a little girl. At home in Beirut, every wall had become a library . . . Whenever you were at home with us, you had a book in your hands. Whenever you weren't there, the books reminded me of your absence. Then my experience of them changed. During the war, when we were being bombed, we'd*

*huddle for shelter in the corridor, pressed against the packed
shelves that lined it from floor to ceiling. Then I started feeling different about them, because there were books I'd see over
and over again, always in the same place, at my eye level. So
from 1979 to 1986 — from when I was eight to when I was fifteen — I could happily look at them. These books were our bar-
ricade, they protected us from the bombs! I spent whole days
and evenings in that passage next to Pable Neruda* (I
Confess That I Have Lived), *Nietzsche* (Beyond Good
and Evil), *Maxime Rodinson* (The Arabs), *Roland Barthes*
(S/Z), *Maurice Blanchot* (Lautréamont and Sade),
Hannah Arendt (The Crisis of Culture), *not to mention the
six fat volumes of the* Robert Dictionary, *1957 edition . . .
From that time on, my relations with books were different.
They switched from being enemies to being my friends and
guardians. I loved them for that. They turned into familiar,
well-intentioned objects. Their presence made me feel safe. All
those books, in fact, I collected them and took them with me to
Paris. I might even read them one day, but in the meantime
they're my talismans!*

ADONIS: How do you account for the fact that books
turned from enemies into friends? What made such a
reversal possible?

*Perhaps it's because I was incapable of domesticating them
myself . . . They had to make the first move. At the time, I
was unable to be dispassionate, I couldn't even open them or
read them . . . So I was rather under their thumb at first, but
this was a good thing in the long run. Their silent presence
finally overcame my resistance.*

You rejected those books, then eventually you accepted them but without reading them. You embraced the idea of the book, not its content. But why couldn't you regard a book as a vision of the world, as a manifesto?

Because I didn't have access to the content. If I'd been older, I too might have been able to cultivate a relationship with them, but the only associations I had were unpleasant ones. I never liked school, and I first met books at school, so they were linked to authority in my mind . . . And yet with all this avoidance of them, and thinking of them as objects I had to compete against, knowledge-filled objects that were bound to seduce and fascinate you – well, by dreading them so much I finally reduced them in my head to harmless objects, familiar but drained of content. They turned into things to be stuck on a shelf, as decoration, nothing more . . . I had to think of some way of minimizing their importance, and it felt comforting to demote them to the status of a chair or a shelf. They were not living beings any more, they were static objects. Some of them had even felt a bit like brothers or sisters, because they'd been created by you (how many books have you published?). And you certainly used to spend more time with them than with me. So what I did was to pretend they didn't exist and assign a new function to them, by redefining them as 'barricades'.

Could one say that, for you, books were associated with the figure of the father?

Yes, that's probably true as well . . . I really don't understand books, and books themselves have never supplied me with any key that would help to decipher them.

Every time you saw your father, he was holding a book, and when your father wasn't there, the book acted as a substitute for him . . . The father and the book were merged into one. So you finally accepted your father, in Beirut?

I suppose so, yes, since the books protected me . . .

And that in its turn encouraged you to accept them?

The books ceased to play their original role. I suppose they tamed me, day by day. I'd pass by in front of them and see that they were still in their places, in the same slot. It meant that if anything got moved about in the bookcases, I'd feel insecure.

Did you feel as if something had been displaced inside you?

They were there, they were reassuring, but I didn't want anyone to mess around with them. They had to remain as they were. So much so that when we left Beirut I brought some of them with me to Paris. Mostly the ones whose spines I knew off by heart.

By so doing, you were somehow fusing your life with books. Making books into an indispensable adjunct of your life from then on . . .

Yes, I was.

And do you still feel that way about them?

When I was little, I hated books and felt embarrassed in front of my school friends that there were so many of them about the house. . . If I invited anyone home, I'd long for the books and paintings on the wall to disappear, because where they lived there weren't any books, or at least not so many. It underlined my difference, it gave me a complex. It made me feel even more of a misfit . . . But it's not like that now. Nowadays I buy books and put them out on my shelves, I still don't read them but I need to have them around, with me, near me. I wander by the bookcase and look at them, checking the titles, and it makes me feel safe! Isn't it silly! I now have a great respect for books, but it's still a slightly fraught relationship, I think; I never feel quite worthy of them, I find it hard to casually pick one up and read it. I force myself to read the stuff I need for my art work, but that's as far as it goes. I feel sure that the minute I open a book to start reading, I won't understand a word; it's like a phobia, I just know in advance that it won't work out. I'm intimidated by books. Recently, and only because of my work, I've been opening some and skimming through a few chapters, telling myself that there's no obligation to read the whole thing and that it's all right too to not understand what's in it . . .

In short, you moved much more in the direction of the school friends you brought home, in front of whom you were ashamed of books, rather than trying to draw them towards you and letting them in on your world . . .

No, I did want to draw them towards me, but there was nowhere in the house that was sufficiently like me.

You say you were attached to books from an early age, so I'm curious to know why you now seem to be more at home with the culture of images, whether it be video, film, photography, installation or performance. How do you make sense of that shift, or that attraction?

It's because I had to create my own identity, my own space, my world for me, separate from yours. That's why images were appealing, and also, perhaps, because we live in a time when images are central to everything. And images seemed somehow more accessible, easier to take in . . .

You lost interest in books. But perhaps you looked for some way of reconciling images with words?

I don't have much of a relationship with words. Ever since arriving in France, I have the feeling that I began to neglect my language-learning . . . And yet at school I used to get top marks in French, English and Arabic. I was hopeless at maths. (Although these days, funnily enough, I love putting numbers in my art work, like in the installation I made in 2003 called Algorhythms. *It plays on the suggestion that there's an equation to be solved by using all the numbers that scroll past.) But since coming to France was like start-ing from scratch, a kind of rebirth, I guess I took the oppor-tunity to focus on what really interested me, which was the visual arts. I'll never perfect my languages by now, there are too many gaps, and to be honest I'm not that motivated. I know I'd never be able to write in any case, not after all the poetry that's been written already, particularly in Arabic, but also in world literature as a whole —*

I've given up on language — there's no chance of my ever becoming an Arabic specialist or any sort of linguist. I now know that my chief working tool will not be language. I've come to terms with this, though it was a wrench! Because while it's true that children always tend to kick against their parents and reject their worlds, deep down inside they long to be like them . . .

The only thing that can be carried across into my art from my relationship with you, from my sense of your intimacy with the Arab tongue and the way you handle it and work it (we'll go back to that in a minute), is a commitment to my own sort of poetry — my storytelling by different means, using images or performances or installations. I do incorporate texts from time to time. The erotic Arab writings of the eleventh, thirteenth and fifteenth centuries, for example. At some point in the future, perhaps I'll even be able to resort creatively to words . . . Just look at this adventure I've got myself into with you, and that will end up as a book, I hope! It's terribly important to me, but I'm starting in softly, with the interview format . . . Because the main goal of the project consisted in spending this time with you, in a face-to-face exchange that can help us get to know each other. And I've opted to do it in French, the language in which I'm most at ease. Whereas if we'd done it in Arabic, the 'boss' would have been you! I'm so happy to have been able to push back my fears about words. I can use words in small doses in my work, but the message is principally conveyed through images and the body. I move between video, performance, installation, objects, dance . . . That's my free-

dom: to be able to select the most appropriate instrument for communicating my thoughts and feelings . . .

This ambiguous relationship of yours with language and words—does it stem from the deficiencies of your education at school, or from being bilingual?

The quick answer would be that being bilingual was not much help. I'd say that speaking two languages instead of one, from infancy onward, eventually forced a choice: I could either be average at both, or else choose one at the expense of the other . . . But given more time to think, I'd say that the most beautiful language in the world for me is Arabic, without the shadow of a doubt. And in the form of poetry, classical or contemporary, it becomes divine. But I was badly taught it . . . Our teachers at school only gave us the austere, rigid side that is the grammar . . . With French, on the other hand, we got literature, and we also got pop music and teenage magazines. It was much more modern and alive. Almost as vivid as English—all my idols were English or American.

And then having parents like you two, with your fault-less Arabic and your ability to make the language even more beautiful, you were a hard act to follow. I told myself I'd never rise to a fraction of your fluency and technical skill . . . Another thing is that here I always speak French, other than at home with you. I speak French even with my Arab friends, it's easier. Lately, though, I've become very interested in bilingualism, because at the end of the day that's where I stand. That's my identity. I'm no longer a proper Arab, or a

Lebanese, and I'm not a proper Frenchwoman either. I belong in neither the French nor the Arabic language. I'm immersed in a 'mongrel', 'creole' speech of which, it so happens, I am a complete master! As it doesn't have any rules, I can make up my own rules one day and trash them the next . . . I'd love to make a film with dialogues in French–Lebanese–English, the 'lingo' you hear in Lebanon and all over the Arab world. I've already experimented with a mini-version of this in a four-minute video called 'La Méprise'. It rehearses an early scene in Jean-Luc Godard's Le Mépris,[1] *in which Brigitte Bardot and Michel Piccoli lovingly list the parts of the body, but adapting it to the 'creole' idiom of French mixed with Lebanese dialect. The effect is to fragment the body even further, since francophone spectators pick up on some 'pieces of the body' while Arabic speakers only recognize the others.*

[LATER . . .]

You gave me my love of things. The earliest was the dining-room table, where the two of you used to sit day after day, for hours on end, on your chairs with a book in front of you . . . At once present and not present . . . I used to gaze at you sitting motionless there, and after a while I couldn't see you any more. All I could see was a table, a lamp, two chairs and a pile of books. Your bodies had dissolved into the chairs! And today, the chair is an element that comes up quite often in my work. Objects took control of your bodies, and ultimately they became more present and real than you were . . .

1 Esber's video feminizes the title of Godard's film (*Contempt*) to mean *The Misunderstanding.* [Trans.]

But to contemplate a thing is also, in a sense, to contemplate oneself. There's an intimate connection between the subject and the self. Indeed, it is impossible to look upon things separately from oneself. I see everything as linked to me, and objects are a part of everyday life. So why do you make that distinction between such objects and the bodies of your father and mother?

Perhaps because it felt as though you were present and absent at the same time. It was a kind of illusion, your bodies were right there in front of me, but like empty shells! The chairs were all there, but you weren't. Especially not you, who travelled a lot. The chair reminded me of you just as the books did . . . You went away, but the chair remained. So I became 'attached' to the chair and to objects in general. And when I discovered, in physics class at school, that matter was a living substance — what a revelation! (Laughter.) Things are alive, they're made of living particles, it made me feel good, I was amazed, and utterly fascinated! A strange relationship between myself and objects took off at that moment. Sometimes I project myself imaginatively into things, they seem so folorn, as though 'lost' in the space of a big room . . . Although they go unnoticed by most people, I can see 'beauty and pride' in them at times. I suspect secret love affairs among the furniture, hearing for instance how the fridge softly purrs to win the heart of the dining-room table . . . I imagine the left-over food returning to the fridge and tantalizing him with descriptions of her glossy wood . . . (Laughter.) Male canaries are not the only ones who sing to call females they've never met, or that they can't see!

You make a distinction between the presence of the book as an object, and the book as a receptacle of knowledge or wisdom . . . What's the difference between these two presences? Does each have a separate existence?

The presence of the chair has no meaning beyond itself. Nothing about it is hidden, it's laid out before you. But where books are concerned, the meaning is two-fold, since a book is both an object and a content (the narrative or the ideas it contains). I managed to form a relationship with the idea of the book, but I couldn't relate to the content. I wasn't old enough to understand it at the time . . .

There might be another reason. A book is, by definition, the bearer of an idea, the author's thought. By the same token you're forced to negotiate with it, as though with another person's opinions, whereas a chair is a blank slate for all the notions you care to pin on it. The chair doesn't carry any meaning 'in advance', and to that extent it's a more inspiring object than a book. And yet it's not unusual for one to 'get through' a book and keep on going, farther than it went itself, because it's made one realize or explore things that are not in it as such. But physical matter, well — you can decide whatever you like about that, can't you?!

I also remember the suffocating silence that hung over our house in those days. I found it thoroughly unnerving! From time to time, if the electricity was working, you used to put on classical records and that was awfully gloomy for a child aged between eight and twelve, like me. During power cuts, the silence was unbroken. Except when any gunshots rang out, signalling the start of another battle. This was good, not only because you were forced to get off your chairs and come crouch in the corridor with my sister and me, but also because here were some exciting sounds at last, some action, some presence, some life! I loved the noise of those bombs even when they went off close by, or landed on our build-ing – that muffled, swelling, mighty noise from the sky became something I almost couldn't do without. The sound of the bombs replaced the sound of your voice. I missed your voice so much! In fact, the days when there were no explo-sions we'd wonder what was going on, it was eerie, like the calm before the storm . . . I domesticated the noises, I'd go: 'that one's landed', 'that one's just been fired', 'there goes a bazooka', 'there goes a cluster bomb', all the time. The first person to guess, just from the noise it made, what kind of missile it was, its trajectory and destination, would try to reassure the others (our family and neighbours, and occa-sional strangers who'd ducked into the first building they saw, to wait until the fighting let up): 'Don't worry, just a Stalin organ fired from a jeep at the bottom of the road, and it's going in such-and-such a direction . . .'

Those noises furnished the space around us, punctuated our days, regulated our outings, our social life, our meals . . . The bombs were what made people come together to sleep and eat as a group. By going to Paris I lost that soundscape, and I miss it enormously. Sometimes I play it back in my head . . .

I remember one night, I must have been four or five, it's one of my earliest memories, you and Mum had lifted me up by the window and were pointing through the glass at some regular but broken trails that gleamed red. These streaks red as neon were tearing full speed through the sky, and dying out . . . It was a lovely colourful show, and I was entranced. You explained that these were shots from a gun, and that when the phosphorescent powder the bullets were stuffed with came into contact with the air, it produced that bright red colour. Later I found out that this kind of ammunition is called a 'tracer bullet', and it's used to indicate the direction of enemy lines . . . They are fired off in automatic mode at night: you chart the luminous path of the bullet and adjust your bursts of machine-gun fire accordingly. Tracer bullets do extra damage because they burn. That was one of my first encounters with colour . . . Weird, isn't it?

Beautiful, actually . . . But didn't you ever wonder about the origins of those bombs? Where they came from, who was dropping them? Did you only think of them as flashes of colour, without caring who the aggressors were, or who were the targets?

No, of course not, but I didn't hold it against the bombs themselves. I did have some degree of political awareness, even at that age. There was no avoiding it, if only to explain why the sky came crashing down on top of us several times a day! One had to take a position, even if the position was to abstain from taking a position . . . In that war you couldn't afford not to be active, on pain of death . . . I knew very well who was attacking whom, and why they were doing it, and naturally I resented the bombers, but not the bombs . . . A bomb is harmless, until someone drops it.

But if they hadn't exploded you wouldn't have heard the sounds you rave about, you wouldn't have seen the colours in the sky . . . What's strange is that notwithstanding the horror, these explosions gave you a pleasurable, aesthetic thrill . . .

They did rather.

How do you account for the way we're able to see a part of beauty in the midst of horror? We must be making a distinction between things that are hateful, such as bombs, and the effects they can produce. September 11, for example, that was a calamity, a human tragedy, a disaster for New York City and its inhabitants. But the destruction of the Twin Towers was a spectacle! Remember how the first plane hit its mark, at a precise height and point of entry, and how the second plane swept in from the other side at a different altitude, and then how each skyscraper crashed to the ground . . . Aesthetically speaking, as spectacles go, this scene was one of the finest man could ever stage. So how do we accomplish the separation between these two things — the human suffering and the visual exhilaration? Is it right to appreciate the beauty for its own sake, in isolation from the rest? What about you, how did you perceive the Beirut war?

Beirut or 9/11, these were horrendous, catastrophic events, full stop! The first time I saw the pictures I had a panic attack, I began shaking and sweating, my teeth were chattering . . . I couldn't speak! Because I could imagine what lay 'outside the frame' of those images. The roar of the plane, the deafening explosion, the screams, the smoke, the shattered glass, the tower swaying from side to side and bursting into flames . . . Because I'd lived through this terror myself in Beirut, we all went through it every time an Israeli plane bombarded the district where we were or the actual building we were in. Except that 9/11 involved a skyscraper and a Boeing, so the horror was ten times greater . . . And on top of everything, after the panic of seeing the pictures, I started thinking about what would happen if the United States hit back!

And yet, in spite of the horror, I've got to admit that it was stunning to watch! We were riveted in front of the telly, as though we'd been hypnotized . . . What a sight! It was magic, pure adrenalin, so exciting, it knocked your senses awake if nothing else!

One thing that consecrated this as a 'spectacle' is the fact that the pictures were broadcast non-stop, for two or three days, on the screens of the whole world. When a town council decides to dynamite some obsolete building or decrepit estate, already that gets coverage on the news. The operation is shown in detail, step by step. Watching buildings collapse obviously has a big attraction for people. On 9/11 I watched this 'spectacular show', but didn't find it beautiful or enthralling straight away. I did so as a self-protective reflex, perhaps . . . It was so harrowing that I was forced to make it beautiful, romantic, crazy and whathaveyou. The first thing I thought, being an unconditional fan of American action movies, was that the Americans had been beaten at their own game, that they'd been left standing . . .

All action films, as a rule – like Independence Day *or anything with Arnold Schwarzenegger in it – are trying to outdo each other in terms of hair-raising stunts and jaw-dropping special effects. And now for the first time we were being treated to some real, unvarnished footage, no wizardry, no makeup . . . For me, exposed to action movies since I was in the cradle, the ante had now been well and truly upped! Ever since then, those old films have begun seeming trite and ropey. It probably means that I've grown up as well* . . . (Smiles.)

Yes, the location and the script were breathtaking. But is it possible to watch such scenes for their colours and sounds alone? Can we enjoy them from an aesthetic point of view, regardless of the reality they represent? Again, we'd necessarily have to divorce the aesthetic side-effects from the criminals who carried out the deed. The same dilemma would arise with, let's say, a thief who directed very beautiful movies, or a murderer who wrote very beautiful poetry. Ought we to approach the poem as an extension of the person who wrote it, and say that this poem is bad because its author is a murderer?

I see what you're driving at, but –

I know, it brings up all sorts of moral issues . . .

Exactly! It can be dangerous, a bit of a slippery slope . . .

So what's the answer, how should we confront these things?

I don't know! It's so complicated . . . What's sure is that there's a massive hypocrisy around this kind of incident. You get people beside themselves with righteous indignation who shriek 'It's appalling! It's disgusting!', precisely because, perhaps, on some level they felt titillated or even enchanted by the spectacle . . . They're scared by their attraction to violence and, what's more, they're so anxious to be seen to be politically correct that they fall over themselves to condemn it . . .

You're not making much sense.

Well, it's all terribly complex, and I think it raises a lot of big questions. One shouldn't rush to judgement on this kind of thing; one should take time to reflect and then speak from experience. One's experience has got to be voiced, I think. In any case, it's not something to be taken lightly, or stirred up with provocative statements. Because some listeners might jump to the wrong conclusions.

Then it can't be discussed openly. In other words, nothing truthful or honest can be said about it, not even as a personal opinion. Society and morality exert a terrific pressure, which it's absolutely impossible to evade . . .

I think it can be discussed, but on one condition: personal involvement. If you were directly affected, if you'd escaped from one of the Towers, for instance, then you'd be entitled to talk about it. No one could disapprove if a Twin Towers survivor were to claim that it was the most momentous experience of his life, the greatest thing that had ever happened to him, that the noise was so mind-blowing it made the wildest rave or decibel-busting techno gig seem like a tea party by comparison!

It's not something you'd say on the day, of course, but later. Back in Lebanon, I often said that the war years were the best time of my life . . . I didn't even mind saying this to people who'd lost relatives or friends. Victims are more readily forgiven, I feel, people make allowances . . . No doubt because victims have a more legitimate right to talk about these dramas, even if it's to go into raptures over them. If you ask me, I don't see how anyone can look back on this kind of calamity without a degree of fascinated excitement. When you're at the very limit of your physical and mental endurance, one shock and you snap into such a state of terror . . . As though your body's exploding from inside, even when you're unhurt. I know how easy it is to get 'hooked' on this heightened sensation, even without being a war professional. It's common knowledge that soldiers or militiamen become addicted to death and often have a hard time coming off it, resuming normal life. But I think this applies to victims too. It took me ten or fifteen years to find a substitute for the adrenalin that flooded through me with every bombardment, every time I looked death in the face. It was difficult to move from a city at war, like Beirut, where you diced with death every day, to a place like Paris where nothing was hap-

pening (bombs-wise, that is!). Of course, you could always become a gangster or a serial killer, a serial rapist, a drugs dealer . . . (Laughter.)

I think I was amazingly lucky to have hung on, to have followed my intuition and clung to the life-raft of art . . . Art may not provide a comparable adrenalin rush, or the same cold sweats, but it's the medium in which I come face to face with myself . . . It has grown into my reason for living. At the age of thirty-three, I've finally found a good reason to get out of bed in the mornings. Before, I always had to think up something to justify each new day.

But why should one be entitled to speak of terrible events only from the insider's position? And never as an outsider? I'm not so sure about that. It all depends. Have I ever told you what happened to Stockhausen?

In relation to 9/11?

There have been no shortage of outpourings on the subject of this attack, all condemning its abject, criminal, fanatical aspects. But there was another side to it that nobody mentioned, namely, that this operation had been the most spectacular action of all time! And this is what Stockhausen said aloud. And he paid very dearly for his words. He was instantly boycotted, and disinvited from a festival where he had been scheduled to appear. This is one of the most eminent composers alive, and he was boycotted!

But if he'd been one of the victims, he could have got away with it.

If he'd been inside, he couldn't have watched it happen . . .

What you've just said reminds me of something so weird. In Lebanon we were experiencing things like that, from the inside. The fact that other people were in a position to describe what they'd seen happen to us – our building being hit by a shell, or our car being attacked by men with Kalashnikovs – turned them into passive voyeurs . . . They became a mirror for us . . .

I doubt it, given that morality, in our society, usually trumps aesthetic considerations. It's very hard to defy moral precepts by speaking one's mind frankly and exercising freedom of thought . . .

Probably, I don't know . . .

The following question therefore arises: should moral rules take precedence over aesthetics?

The trouble with aesthetics is that it's a very relative concept, which can open the door to frightful distortions . . . In the name of a 'particular notion of beauty' and on behalf of a particular notion of racial perfection or purity, the Nazis exterminated millions, Jews, Gypsies –

Not so much in the name of aesthetics as in that of ideology, surely?

Of ideology, of course, but they put out books that explained how to recognize a Jew by his physical characteristics, with the help of little drawings. And there was a whole fascist aesthetic expressed in the mass rallies, the uniforms, the architecture . . . The aesthetic can therefore be dangerous . . .

Indeed it can. And horrific acts can equally well be committed in the name of morality. Morality is often reactionary. It often brushes individual liberties aside to lay down rules that are irksome, intolerable and inhuman.

Yes, like the Taliban for instance.

Yes. A specific moral code can be invoked to destroy a whole society, destroy its humanity, annihilate a culture or an entire civilization.

Like during the Middle Ages, when the Church had such exhorbitant power, or during the time of the Inquisition in Europe (with the trials of witches and wise men), or in South America (when white settlers slaughtered the indigenous population).

All in all it's a delicate question, that remains unresolved . . .

[LATER . . .]

You were often away, you used to go off and teach in the United States or France, you were forever on a lecture tour or a trip . . . But even when you were around, you were absent. Endlessly elusive, absorbed by your world, your dreams or whatever it was . . . You forced me to seek you in things, in people, for I never could read your work . . . I'd suddenly get cold feet at the thought of finding you by that route, because I didn't want to come across the poet, I wanted to know the father first. With you my relationship was one of absence within presence . . . It forced me, or encouraged me, to take an interest in Sufi mysticism. For in the poetry of Ibn Arabi2 and of al-Hallaj (I'm not so keen on Rumi3), there's a similar tension between the seen and the unseen . . . I had to find an explanation for your invisibility, I had to restore you to reality, the reality of daily life. That's why I prefer dreams and the more intangible things . . . It's an attempt to see beyond the material, beyond appearances. To not take things for granted. And to be in constant flux, therefore, in an endless search for meaning, for presence, for absolutes . . . And this informs my work, I keep coming back to that, don't I, it's my mainstay these days . . . Your advice was always: 'Don't run after people, because people change their minds and their allegiances. You must be the hub around which others revolve.' I always found that impossible, pretentious and rather 'monkish', but now I'm constructing myself, building my hub. You've managed at long last to push me beyond settling for what is given . . .

And you never wondered about the reasons for my absence and my presence? Didn't you ever wonder why I was so often away?

I don't remember.

2 Ibn Arabi (?–1240): poet born in Murcia who died in Damascus. Considered to be the greatest Arab-Muslim mystic.

3 Rumi (1207–73): Persian poet and leading Muslim mystic.

You never asked yourself the question? It never occurred to you that there might have been difficulties at home?

No, it didn't! I was too little to pick up on that . . .

You didn't worry about such things?

No, never, how could I have guessed, I lacked the experience . . .

Because these things don't happen out of the blue. If someone spends so much time away, there must be reasons, a bad atmosphere at home, a problem of some sort . . .

Well, yes . . . But I couldn't have registered that at the time. If I weigh up everything now, and fit it all together, I guess that's probably the reason why I make art. The deprivations that marked my childhood also strengthened my personality, and made me into someone who dares 'lay claim' to art. I'm not sure how else to put it . . . That time is behind me now, and I've 'worked on myself', as they say. I know that I didn't receive enough affection, and that I lack self-confidence, but that's what empowers me to create. Because for me creativity is a gift, a huge stroke of luck. If I didn't have that, my life would be dreadful.

It's very important. But does what you were talking about allow you to work in bursts, according to your circumstances and moods? Or does it compel you to elaborate a genuine universe, a world all your own?

My 'world', this world of my own, is created as I go along ... It can't pop up fully formed all by itself.

Very true, but still there has to be something in a person's heart, in his guts, in his mind, something that haunts him and shadows his steps ...

Something, yes, but one can't know what that is. It's not apparent in advance. I mean, I often find myself making something (a video or a photograph) that surprises even me ... I can see something new in it, a new element has come into my world, and that's great!

Yes, it's just a matter of time ... To return to your question: do you really think that our childhood experiences have a greater influence on our life choices than our subsequent encounters with culture or with people?

Childhood can certainly become a burden ... Without experiences, without the people we meet who spark off memories and echoes, childhood in itself is a bit of a drag. For me, it's the contact with others and the experiences of everyday life that cast new light on one's childhood — only then does it get more interesting. Otherwise, it's a dead weight ... The experiences life brings us and the people we meet are what turn childhood from an inert stretch of the past, lifeless and nostalgic, into a worthwhile present and future ...

[LATER ...]

I know that my artistic world doesn't particularly interest you; you don't think there's enough 'art' to it. Although you

216

said once that my films were like poems, and I realized then that I was trying to create my own form of poetry. I also like to occupy space, use the body and the voice, deploy everyday objects within a mise en scène, and create new spaces that might be imaginary, unstable or in a process of mutation. I love the world of animals, spiders and insects. And yet I grew up surrounded by artists: all your friends, if they weren't poets, writers, critics or philosophers, were painters or sculptors. You hardly knew any film-makers or musicians, or at any rate very few musicians who were into anything but traditional music. You, as a poet, have worked to modernize Arabic poetry, but the painters and sculptors you surround yourself with are so dreary and classical! All those abstract canvases layered with 'matter', those 'powerful', 'subtle', 'sensitive' palettes, expressing 'all the poetry and pain of exile' or reinventing the cultural heritage of Ancient-Egypt-cum-Babylon with lashings of cuneiform script, when it's not 'The Desert World of the Bedouins' or 'The Traditional Architecture of Ancient Arab Towns'. Then we have the ones who shamelessly rip off early twentieth-century European masters – Matisse–Miró–Picasso–Chagall–Klee–Kandinsky–Tapiès–Bacon for the painters, Brancusi–Giacometti–Moore for the sculptors. I got fed up with the sight of countless paintings in which it was impossible to feel the artist's uniqueness, since they were all interchangeable. In the same way, the texts by Arab art critics could apply just as well to any and all of these painters! There are honourable exceptions, of course: a handful of artists with an unmistakable style of their own and an almost physical,

4 Marwan Kassab Bachi (b. 1934): one of the greatest contemporary Syrian painters. Having taken German nationality, he lives and works in Berlin.

spiritual commitment to their art (people like Marwan[4]). But the rest seemed to lack body — there was no innovation, no risk-taking, no political engagement, no clear standpoint in relation to the world . . . And at the same time these painters aspired to become poets, writers, art critics and whathaveyou. How on earth was I supposed to take my cue from all this? It bored me from the word go. Deep down I was unconsciously telling myself that there must be, or there'd better be, something else, some other form of art-making. As soon as I arrived in France, I discovered dance theatre: Pina Bausch (Arwad took me to see her in 1990), a modern Japanese Butoh troupe called Sankai Juku, and plays by Bob Wilson. And then one day on a visit to New York, again with Arwad, we went to see a performance artist called Claude Wampler. I was utterly transfixed! I thought: 'This is it!' It was a revelation. I don't know what that woman has gone on to do, but seeing her was absolutely seminal for me. And it was also with Arwad that I used to watch the videos she chose from the rental shop in Beirut during the war, Fellini, Pasolini, Hitchcock, and odd things like Emil Loteanu's Gypsies Go to Heaven, *which was the inspiration behind one of my first video performances . . . All those images are etched into me, and played their part in the construction of my world. After those first eye-openers, my ideas were developed further by my studies and by the teachers I found, who guided me towards the art of today. I felt ever more distanced from all those painter friends of the family, as I realized that here was the alternative I'd been looking for all along: it's what is known as 'contemporary art'.*

That's an autobiographical account that sheds clear light on your aesthetic tastes and relationship with art. But when you say 'classical art', what are you referring to?

I'm not necessarily speaking with scientific precision, and 'classicism' of course means something different in art-historical terms. When I say 'classical' I mean conventional, run-of-the-mill art, the kind of thing everyone does, stuff you see everywhere . . . Not without subtle differences, i.e. this one inclines to 'constructivism' whereas the other is a bit of a 'cubist', and the next is more into 'this' or 'that'. Perhaps it's also that I'd have expected something a lot more impressive from friends of yours, something as spectacular as what you have done for – or with – classical Arab poetry. I may not have read you but I know that you've modernized our poetry, that you've broken new ground, and that the painters and sculptors in our circle were doing nothing of the kind. Their works used to bore me to death! They still do . . . I saw painters churning out the same old pictures, sculptors hacking out the same old sculptures. Though I hadn't begun my artistic education in those days, and my eye was untrained, their work didn't excite me. It didn't nourish me. It was dull . . . And what I needed was to be surprised, I needed to dream . . .

Yes, but when you're looking at this modern Arab art, what do you judge it by? Do you evaluate it in its own terms as such, or in relation to other expressions which you have, or had, in mind?

I evaluate and judge it in terms of the issues that mattered to me as a teenager during the war. With the eyes of some-one who hungered for dreams and knowledge, who was avid for Life. So these pieces struck me as stale and old-fashioned, the painting of an earlier generation. And yet it can't, I don't think, be reduced to a generational problem, because now, more than ever, these paintings have nothing to say to me . . .

Epilogue

I've always seen space as unstable and ephemeral. A reflection of the space created by chaos and war. We never know whether a bomb is about to fall on us or on the people next door, to obliterate our space or the space of others. Will we lose an arm, will we lose a leg?

Closing the shutters, dragging the mattresses into the passage or against the windows, crouching as we enter the kitchen in case of snipers. A space invaded by the militia or by the occupying army. A space annexed, a space destroyed. An unstable, fragile space.

'Unstable presence: yours, the others.' In my actions/performances, I attempt to dominate unstable spaces: recasting them, occupying them with my body and with objects (chairs, ropes, mats, ladders, lamps; threatening objects that are sharp or pointed). I come to redefine them in a bid to tame the unstable and the ephemeral.

The creation of a new, mutant space which I furnish with things, stories, presences and especially absences. Reticence, seduction (so as to lure others into my space, hence my love of spiders). My body placed under observation, motionless body, body that will be observing back nonetheless.

When a stray bullet flies into a room, there's no telling where it came from, and along what path it will pierce what, or whom . . . It may come in through the ceiling, through the right-angle of the window, through the far corner or from any odd, unprecedented spot. This stray bullet or piece of shrapnel abruptly alerts us to the existence of point X, exactly two centimetres from the door to the left. A point that has never existed before, that has never been seen, whose existence had never even been suspected . . .

Projectiles of every sort, bullets, bombs and body parts, trace figures through people's public and private space. They constitute an unexpected invasion that defies the laws of gravity and architecture.

I believe this type of chaos left an indelible imprint on me. It gave me the urge and the need to produce tense (and unpredictable) forms in makeshift spaces, preserving the nature of a form in suspense . . .

It's hard to tell whether this is an action that's just beginning, just ending or somewhere in the middle. People fidget as they wait. The ensuing tension is shared with the spectators.